NIKON D5500

THE EXPANDED GUIDE

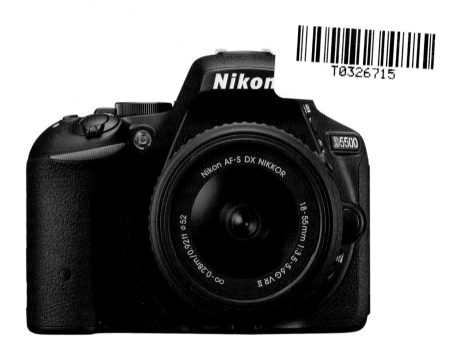

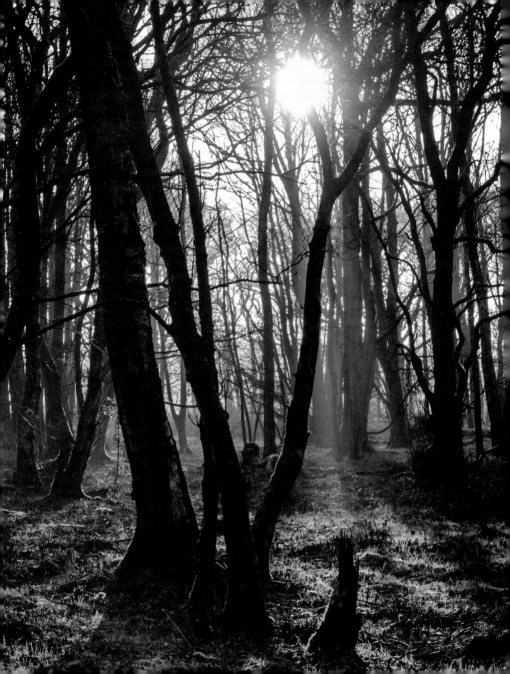

NIKON D5500

THE EXPANDED GUIDE

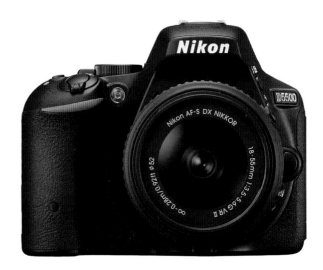

Jon Sparks

AMMONITE
PRESS

First published 2015 by
Ammonite Press
an imprint of AE Publications Ltd
166 High Street, Lewes, East Sussex, BN7 1XU, UK

Text © AE Publications Ltd, 2015
Images © Jon Sparks 2015 (unless otherwise specified)
Copyright © in the Work AE Publications Ltd, 2015

ISBN 978-1-78145-208-0

British Library Cataloging in Publication Data: A catalog
record of this book is available from the British Library.

Editor: Rob Yarham
Series Editor: Richard Wiles
Design: Richard Dewing Associates

Typefaces: Giacomo
Color reproduction by GMC Reprographics
Printed in China

《 PAGE 2
MISTY WOOD
The D5500 can deliver excellent
image quality even under difficult
conditions, and this book will help
you make the most of it.
70mm, 1/60 sec., f/14,
ISO 160, tripod.

» CONTENTS

1 OVERVIEW

The D5500 is the latest model in Nikon's advanced "consumer" series, occupying a middle position in the DX-format camera range, between the entry-level D3300 and the "enthusiast/semi-pro" D7200. The D5XXX series were the first Nikon digital SLRs to have an articulating rear screen (recently joined by the full-frame D750). This offers extra flexibility when using Live View and especially when shooting movies. The D5500 adds touch-control to this screen.

Nikon has always valued continuity as well as innovation—for instance, it has retained its tried and tested F lens-mount (originally introduced in 1959). This means it's possible to use many classic Nikon lenses with the latest digital SLRs (DSLRs) like the D5500, although care is needed and some camera functions (e.g. autofocus) may be lost (see Chapter 7, page 188).

Nikon's first digital SLR was the 1.3-megapixel E2s. It had no rear screen and images could only be viewed by connecting it to an external device. A far more practical introduction was the 2.7 megapixel D1, in 1999. Arguably the most influential digital camera ever launched, the D1 was the first DSLR to approach the flexibility and ease of handling of 35mm film SLRs. The D1's sensor adopted the DX format (see page 10), subsequently used in every Nikon DSLR until the "full-frame" (FX) D3 in 2008.

INTO THE BLUE »
When you unpack a new camera, it's tempting to start shooting right away—and taking pictures is the best way to learn. However, it still makes sense to peruse this book first, to ensure you don't miss out on new features and functions.
92mm, 1/30 sec., f/5.6, ISO 800.

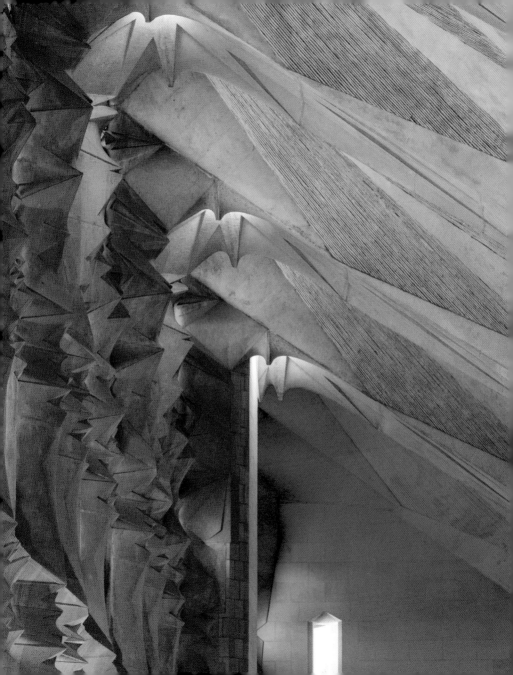

1 › Continuing evolution

In 2004, Nikon introduced their first "enthusiast" DSLR, the six-megapixel D70; its direct descendants were the D80 (2006) and then the D90 (2008), but by then the range had diversified further, with a new "entry-level" series beginning with the D40 (2006); this was followed by the D60 (2008) and then by the D3000, D3100, D3200, and D3300.

Meanwhile, the D90 was one of Nikon's most significant launches—a range of new features was overshadowed by one headline-grabber as it became the first DSLR capable of shooting video. The D90 remained on sale (and indeed is still listed today) even as many of its innovations were incorporated into the D5000 (2009), which added a fold-out LCD screen. The D5100 (2011) had more pixels, a smaller overall form factor, and a repositioned screen pivot. The D5200 (early 2013) added refinements including a 24-megapixel sensor, enhanced image processing and an upgraded autofocus system. Less than a year later, the D5300 became Nikon's first DSLR with onboard Wi-Fi and GPS.

Nikon continues to roll out new models in this range on a regular basis, but it's notable that there was no D5400, suggesting that they would like us to see the D5500 as a bigger step forward. The D5500 is lighter and slimmer than its predecessors, but functionally quite similar, apart from the addition of a touch screen and the removal of the built-in GPS.

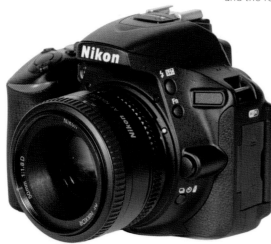

Nikon D5500

Nikon D1 (1999)
The D1 was a revolutionary camera, making digital photography a practical, everyday proposition for thousands of professionals, not to mention amateur "early adopters".

Nikon D70 (2004)
The D70 was the camera that first persuaded a host of enthusiasts and not a few professionals (including the author) to take the plunge into digital photography.

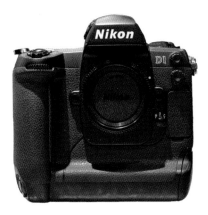

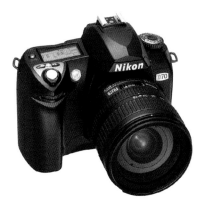

Nikon D90 (2008)
The D90 had many new features, but one of these grabbed all the headlines as it became the first DSLR capable of shooting video.

Nikon D5000 (2009)
The D5000's main innovation was its articulating screen, establishing the basic design cues for subsequent models.

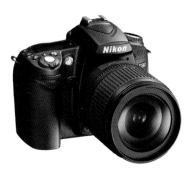

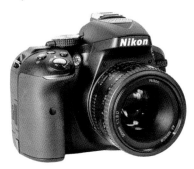

1 > About the Nikon D5500

At first glance, the D5500 may look like a modest upgrade to the D5300, but there are several visible changes, and more hidden under the surface. The camera is a fraction smaller and lighter than its predecessors, thanks to the use of innovative carbon fiber-reinforced thermoplastics for structural elements of the body. The shallower body makes the handgrip more pronounced, giving a more secure hold for almost all users.

The D5500 has a 24-megapixel sensor, like the D5200 and D5300. Between these two models, Nikon dispensed with an "anti-aliasing" filter in front of the sensor. The first Nikon to do away with the AA filter was the D800e, but the D7100 soon followed, and the trend continues in the D5500. The effect should be to make images even sharper, and results do seem to bear this out—but the difference will only really show up with good lenses and good technique. The D5500 also uses the latest EXPEED 4 image processing system.

The D5500 retains the onboard Wi-Fi capabilities introduced on the D5300, but dispenses with that model's onboard GPS.

Like all Nikon SLRs the D5500 is part of a vast system of lenses, accessories, and software. The Expanded Guide to the Nikon D5500 will guide you through all aspects of the camera's operation, and its relation to the system as a whole.

> Nikon DX-format sensors

DX-format sensors, measuring approximately 23.6 x 15.8mm (with slight variations), were used in every Nikon DSLR from the D1 onward, until the arrival of "full-frame" or FX-format cameras (e.g. the D4, D800, and D750). The sensors in these models are approximately 36 x 24mm. The D5500's sensor measures 23.5 x 15.6 mm, making it fractionally smaller than some other models, though a millimeter here or there is of no real significance.

The number of pixels on the sensor has risen from 2.7 million on the D1 to around 24 million across the current DX range. Early models used CCD sensors but today CMOS (Complementary Metal Oxide Semiconductor) sensors are used in all of Nikon's DSLRs.

The DX format dictates a 1.5x crop factor (see page 191), relative to the same lenses used on 35mm and FX cameras. Its 24 million pixels produce images at a native size of 6000 x 4000 pixels, making them suitable for demanding large prints, as well as book and magazine reproduction; dispensing with an anti-aliasing (optical low-pass) filter helps sharpness still further.

FOCUSING ON THE DETAILS »
Twenty-four million pixels are more than enough to deliver crisp detail for almost any purpose— but good lenses and technique are important. *35mm, 0.4 sec., f/11, ISO 100, tripod.*

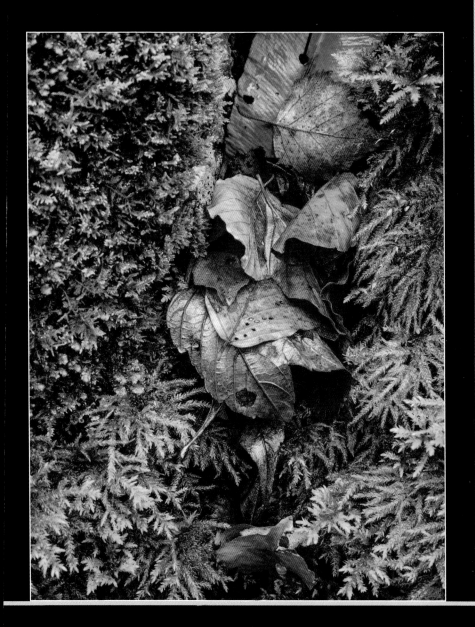

1 » MAIN FEATURES OF THE NIKON D5500

Sensor

24.2 effective megapixel DX-format RGB CMOS sensor measuring 23.5 x 15.6mm and producing maximum image size of 6000 x 4000 pixels; self-cleaning function. No optical low-pass (anti-aliasing) filter.

Image processor

EXPEED 4 image processing system featuring 14-bit analog-to-digital (A/D) conversion with 16-bit image processing.

Focus

Nikon Multi-CAM 4800DX autofocus module featuring 39 autofocus points. Three focus modes: (S) Single-servo AF; (C) Continuous-servo AF; (M) Manual focus. Three AF-area modes: Single-area AF; Dynamic-area AF with option of 3D tracking; Auto-area AF. Rapid focus point selection and focus lock.

ISO

ISO range between 100 and 25,600. Exposure compensation between −5 Ev and +5 Ev; exposure lock and exposure bracketing facility.

Exposure modes

Two fully auto modes: auto; auto (flash off). Sixteen Scene modes: Portrait; Landscape; Child; Sports; Close up; Night portrait; Night landscape; Party/indoor; Beach/ snow; Sunset; Dusk/dawn; Pet portrait; Candlelight; Blossom; Autumn colors; Food. Ten Effects modes: Night Vision; Super Vivid; Pop; Photo Illustration; Toy camera effect; Miniature Effect; Selective Color; Silhouette; High key; Low key. Four user-controlled modes: (P) Programmed auto with flexible program; (A) Aperture-priority auto; (S) Shutter-priority auto; (M) Manual.

Shutter

Shutter speeds from 1/4000 sec. to 30 sec., plus B and T. Maximum continuous frame advance 5fps.

Release modes

Single Frame; Continuous L; Continuous H; Quiet shutter release; Self-timer; Delayed remote; Quick response remote.

Viewfinder

Pentamirror viewfinder with 95% coverage and 0.82x magnification.

LCD monitor

Touch-sensitive vari-angle 3.2in./81mm, 1037k-dot TFT LCD display with 100% frame coverage.

Movie mode

Movie capture in .MOV format (MPEG compression) with image size (pixels) of: 1920 x 1280; 1280 x 720; 640 x 424.

Buffer

Buffer capacity allows up to 100 frames (JPEG basic, large) to be captured in a continuous burst at 5fps, approximately eight RAW files.

Built-in flash

Pop-up flash (manually activated) with Guide Number of 12 (m) or 39 (ft) at ISO 100; supports i-TTL balanced fill-flash for DSLR (when matrix or center-weighted metering is selected) and Standard i-TTL flash for DSLR (when spot metering is selected). Five flash-sync modes: Standard (front-curtain) flash mode (labeled "auto" or "fill flash" according to operating mode); Slow sync; Rear-curtain sync; Red-eye reduction; Red-eye reduction with slow sync. Flash compensation from −3 to +1 Ev.

Custom functions

21 parameters and elements of the camera's operations can be customized through the Custom setting menu.

File formats

The D5500 supports NEF (RAW) (12- or 14-bit) and JPEG (Fine/Normal/Basic) file formats, plus .MOV movie format.

Storage

Secure Digital (SD) card slot; accepts SDHC and SDXC cards.

System back-up

Compatible with over 60 current and many non-current Nikkor lenses (functionality varies with older lenses); SB-series flashguns; Wireless Remote Control ML-L3 and WR-R10; ME-1 stereo microphone; and many more Nikon system accessories.

Connectivity

Onboard Wi-Fi. Connectors for external microphone, USB/AV, HDMI and Nikon remote cords/wireless controllers.

Software

Supplied with Nikon View NX2 (incorporates Nikon Transfer 2); compatible with Nikon Capture NX-D and many third-party imaging applications.

1 » FULL FEATURES AND CAMERA LAYOUT

FRONT OF CAMERA

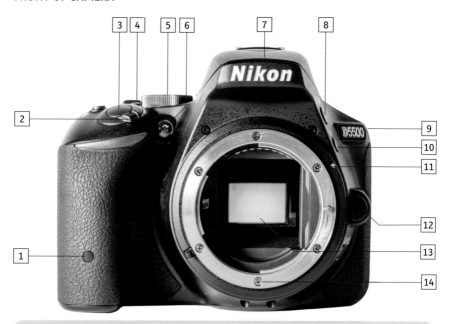

1	Infrared receiver (front)	10	Fn button
2	Power switch	11	Mounting mark
3	Shutter-release button	12	Lens-release button
4	Live View switch	13	Mirror
5	Mode dial	14	Lens mount
6	AF-assist illuminator/Self-timer/Red-eye reduction lamp		
7	Built-in flash		
8	Flash/Flash mode/Flash compensation button		
9	Left strap mount		

BACK OF CAMERA

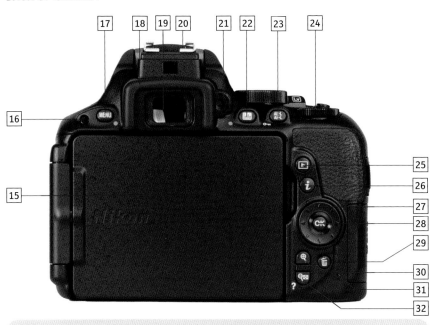

15 Vari-angle monitor	26 *i* button
16 Infrared receiver (rear)	27 Multi-selector
17 MENU button	28 OK button
18 Eyecup	29 Delete button
19 Viewfinder eyepiece	30 Playback zoom in button
20 Accessory hotshoe cover	31 Memory card access lamp
21 Diopter adjustment dial	32 Thumbnail/playback zoom out/Help button
22 Info button	
23 AE-L/AF-L/Protect button	
24 Command dial	
25 Playback button	

1 » FULL FEATURES AND CAMERA LAYOUT

TOP OF CAMERA   **LEFT SIDE**

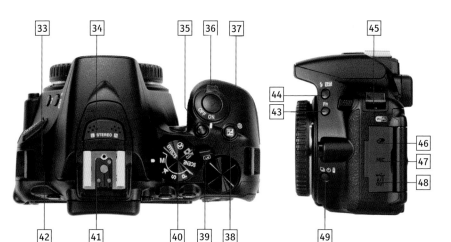

33	Speaker	41	Accessory hotshoe
34	Stereo microphone	42	Focal plane mark
35	Movie-record button		
36	Power switch		
37	Shutter-release button		
38	Exposure compensation / Aperture adjustment/ Flash compensation button		
39	Live View switch		
40	Mode dial		

43	Fn button
44	Flash/Flash mode/Flash compensation button
45	Camera strap mount
46	Accessory terminal beneath cover
47	External microphone connector beneath cover
48	USB and AV connector beneath cover
49	Release Mode/Self-timer/Remote control

BOTTOM OF CAMERA

RIGHT SIDE

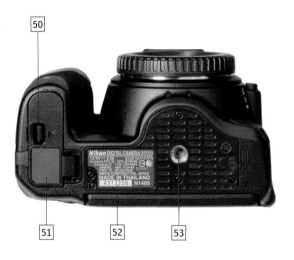

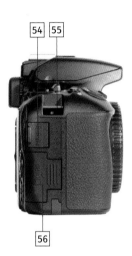

50	Battery compartment release lever
51	Battery compartment
52	Camera serial number
53	Tripod socket (¼in.)

54	HDMI connector cover
55	Right strap mount
56	Memory card slot cover

1 » INFORMATION DISPLAY

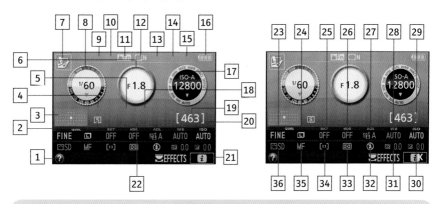

1	Help icon	
2	Release mode	
3	AF-area mode indicator/Focus point	
4	Autoexposure (AE) lock indicator	
5	Bracketing indicator	
6	Aperture (f-number)	
7	Shooting mode	
8	Shutter speed	
9	Satellite signal indicator	
10	WiFi connection indicator/Eye-Fi connection indicator	
11	Touch Fn assignment	
12	Vignette control indicator	
13	Exposure delay mode	
14	Date stamp indicator	
15	Flash control indicator	
16	Battery indicator	
17	ISO sensitivity	
18	ADL bracketing amount	
19	Exposures remaining/White balance recording/Capture mode indicator	

20	"K" (when over 1000 exposures remain)
21	Info icon
22	Exposure/Exposure compensation/ Bracketing progress indicator
23	Image quality
24	Image size
25	Auto bracketing
26	HDR indicator
27	Active D-Lighting
28	White balance
29	ISO sensitivity
30	Exposure compensation
31	Flash compensation
32	Flash mode
33	Metering
34	AF-area mode
35	Focus mode
36	Picture control

» VIEWFINDER DISPLAY

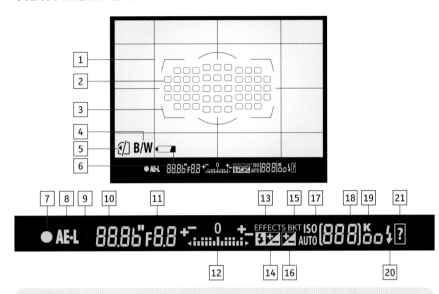

1 Framing grid	**12** Exposure indicator/ exposure compensation display/ electronic rangefinder	**18** Number of exposures remaining/number of exposures remaining in buffer/white balance recording indicator/ exposure compensation value/ flash compensation value/ ISO sensitivity/capture mode indicator
2 Focus points		
3 AF area brackets		
4 Monochrome indicator	**13** Special effects mode indicator	
5 No memory card warning	**14** Flash compensation indicator	
6 Low battery warning	**15** Bracketing indicator	
7 Focus indicator	**16** Exposure compensation indicator	
8 AE lock indicator	**17** Auto ISO sensitivity indicator	**19** "K" (when over 1000 exposures remain)
9 Flexible program indicator		**20** Flash-ready indicator
10 Shutter speed		**21** Warning indicator
11 Aperture		

The Nikon D5500 sports over a dozen control buttons, a mode dial, a command dial, and a multi-selector. This plethora of controls can seem overwhelming, so it's important to realize that you don't have to master them all at once. The D5500 can be used as simply as any "point-and-shoot" camera, though giving far superior image quality. It arrives set to its simplest operating mode—^{AUTO} 📷 —and you can revert to it at any time.

You can also quickly reset virtually all other camera settings to the initial default by holding down **MENU** and **info** (marked with green dots) for at least 2 seconds; this is known as a two-button reset.

However, all those buttons and dials are an outward sign of the camera's imaging power and versatility. Leaving it at default settings misses out on much of this potential. To make a start without getting bogged down in too many options, the key is understanding which modes and which settings are suited to your photography. A great way in is by exploring the Scene modes (see pages 42–55).

You can, of course, minimize use of buttons and dials by using the D5500's touch screen wherever possible (see page 32). This will feel more familiar if you're used to a smartphone or tablet. However, this is simply an alternative (and sometimes considerably slower) way of accessing the same range of options.

This chapter will cover the location and use of the main controls and explore the main shooting modes and other functions. Chapter 3 delves into the menus in detail (see page 110).

LOW LIGHT　　　　　　　　　　　　**»**
The D5500 performs well in a wide range of situations, including low light. While its default settings will usually produce acceptable images, you will need to explore its functions more fully to achieve the best results.
70mm, 1/125 sec., f/6.3, ISO 800.

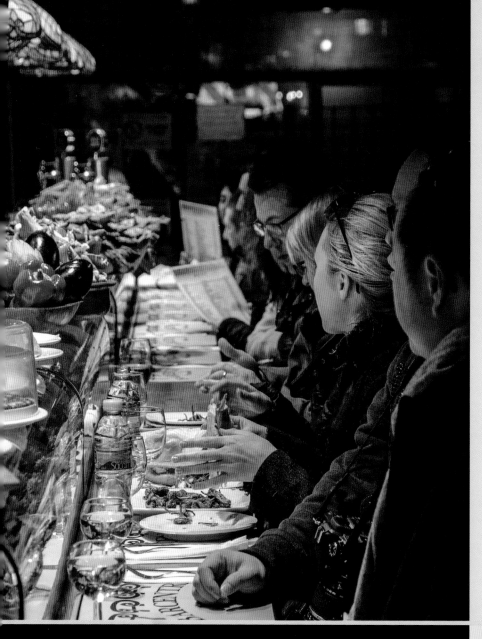

When first switched on, the camera prompts you to set language, time, date, and time zone (see under Setup menu, page 128). A few other steps, like charging the battery and inserting a memory card, are also required before you can use the camera.

› Inserting and removing the battery

The camera is supplied with an EN-EL14a li-ion rechargeable battery. Invert the camera and locate the battery compartment, below the handgrip. Release the latch to open it. Insert the battery, contacts first, with the face that says "Nikon" facing away from the camera. Nudge the gold-colored latch aside, then slide the battery in gently until the latch clicks home. Close the compartment cover.

To remove the battery, switch off the camera, and open the compartment cover. Press the gold latch to release the battery and gently remove it.

INSERTING THE BATTERY ≈

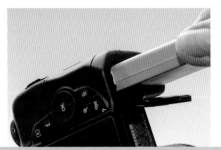

› Charging the battery

Use the supplied MH-24 charger, plugged into a mains outlet, to charge the battery. A full charge/recharge takes around 110 minutes. Remove the battery terminal cover (if attached) and insert the battery into the charger with "Nikon" uppermost and terminals facing the contacts on the charger. Press gently into position. The orange lamp blinks while the battery is charging, then shines steadily when charging is complete.

Battery life

Battery life depends on various factors. The LCD screen, the built-in flash, and the autofocus motors in lenses all draw power from the battery. Long meter-off delays reduce battery life. Extensive Live View/movie shooting is particularly draining. Extreme cold can also reduce battery life.

Under stringent test conditions (CIPA) the D5500 delivers around 820 shots before the battery needs recharging. However, if you shoot using the viewfinder, focus manually and minimize screen use (e.g. changing settings, reviewing shots), you may achieve several thousand shots per charge.

The battery icon in the information display shows roughly how much charge remains. It blinks when the battery is exhausted, and a warning also appears in the viewfinder.

For information on alternative power-sources, see Chapter 8 (page 214).

› Inserting and removing memory cards

The D5500 stores images on Secure Digital (SD) cards, including SDHC and SDXC cards. See page 216 for more about memory cards.

Inserting a memory card
1) Switch off the camera. If the access lamp on the camera back (below the multi-selector) is blinking, images are being written to the card. Wait till it goes off.

2) Slide the card slot cover (lower right side of camera) rearward. It will spring open.

3) To remove a memory card, press it gently into its slot—it springs out slightly. You can now remove it.

4) Insert a card with its label facing the rear and the "cut-off" corner facing into the slot. Gently push the card into the slot until it clicks home. The access lamp will light briefly.

5) Close the card slot cover.

› Formatting a memory card

You'll need to format new memory cards, or ones that have been used in another camera, before using them with the D5500. In everyday use, formatting is the speediest way to erase images so you can reuse the card—but make sure the images have been saved elsewhere first.

1) Press **MENU**. Select **Setup menu** on the left of the screen. You can use the multi-selector or the touch screen.

2) Tap **Format memory card**, or select it and press (OK).

3) Select **Yes** and press (OK). Or tap **Yes** and tap again to confirm.

INSERTING A MEMORY CARD ⌄

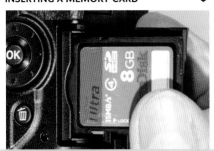

FORMATTING A MEMORY CARD ⌄

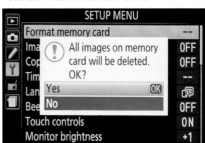

› Attaching the strap

Attach either end of the strap to the appropriate eyelet, at top left and right sides of the camera. Loosen the strap where it runs through the buckle, then pass the end of the strap through the eyelet and back through the buckle. Bring the end of the strap back through the buckle, under the length of strap already threaded. Repeat on the other side. Adjust the length as required, leaving a good "tail" for security, then tighten the strap to leave it snug and tidy. See page 210 for notes on alternative straps.

STRAP ⟱
The strap is shown fully tightened on the right, threaded but not yet tightened on the left. This method is not the same as that shown in the Nikon manual, but is neater and more secure.

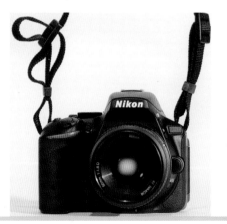

› Adjusting for eyesight

The D5500 allows you to tune the viewfinder optics to your individual eyesight: essential for the clearest possible view. The diopter adjustment dial is just right of the viewfinder. Half-press the shutter-release button to activate the viewfinder readouts, then rotate the dial until they appear sharpest.

The range of dioptric adjustment is between -1.7 and $+0.5$ m^{-1}. If you wear glasses or contact lenses for distance vision, keep them on/in when adjusting the diopter (and whenever you use the viewfinder).

DIOPTER ADJUSTMENT DIAL ⟱

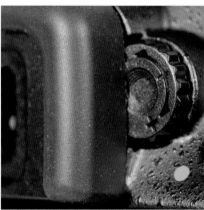

› Mounting lenses

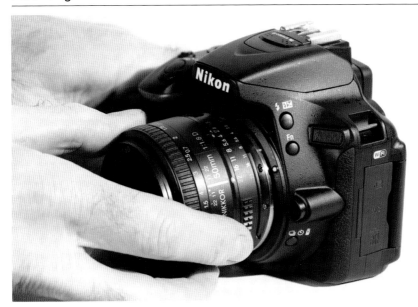

Switch the camera off. Remove the camera body cap or lens if already mounted. To remove a lens, press the lens-release button and turn the lens clockwise (as you face the front of the camera).

To mount a lens, remove its rear cap. Align the index mark on the lens with the white dot on the camera body. Insert the lens into the camera and turn it anti-clockwise until it clicks home. Do not use force—a correctly aligned lens will mount smoothly.

See Chapter 7 (page 188) for information on compatible lenses.

Warning!

Replace the lens or body cap immediately. Don't touch the electrical contacts on the lens or camera body. Dirty contacts can cause malfunctions.

2 » BASIC CAMERA FUNCTIONS

With strap, lens, battery, and memory card on board, the D5500 is ready to shoot. The camera arrives set to 🅰 Auto mode and with its LCD screen stowed away. The D5500 will happily shoot indefinitely like this, but as soon as you want to change any settings, review, or playback your shots, use Live View, or shoot movies, you'll need to use the screen and its information.

As you begin to explore a wider range of options, the key controls are the mode dial, command dial, and multi-selector, along with the release mode button. With the D5500, for the first time on a Nikon DSLR, you also have the option of using the touch screen.

In Auto and Scene modes, it is perfectly possible to shoot without making use of any of these controls, although this is not necessarily recommended.

› Switching the camera on

The power switch surrounds the shutter-release button. It has two self-explanatory settings: OFF and ON.

› Operating the shutter

The shutter-release button operates in two stages. Pressing it lightly, until you feel initial resistance, activates the metering and focus functions. Half-pressure also clears the information display, menus, or image playback, making the D5500 fully ready to shoot. Press the button more firmly (but still smoothly) to take the picture.

> **Tip**
>
> *If you inadvertently turn the power switch OFF while the camera is still recording image(s), you won't lose them. The camera will finish the process before turning off. Just be sure not to remove the memory card (pages 23 and 216) until the process is complete.*

POWER SWITCH AND SHUTTER RELEASE ⌄

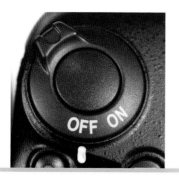

› Using the LCD screen

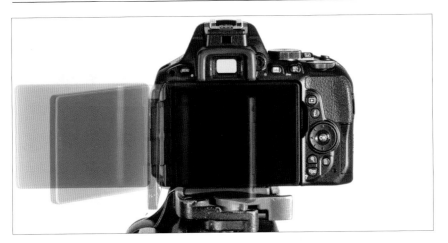

A RANGE OF SCREEN POSITIONS ☆

To use the screen, grasp its right edge and ease it away from the camera. The screen can be angled and rotated to a wide range of positions, including a forward-facing position for "selfies", but it is self-evidently more vulnerable to damage when opened out. For normal use, open the screen out, rotate it 180° (push the top away from you) then fold it back against the camera body until it clicks into place.

It's convenient to leave the screen in this position, but it is open to scratches and other damage. It's safer to stow the screen away when transporting or storing the camera. If you set a suitable shooting mode

beforehand, you can grab shots quickly, if the need arises, without delaying to open out the screen first.

For more on using the screen's touch functions, see page 32.

> ### Tip
>
> *The screen can be hard to see clearly in bright sunlight. Changing the angle may help. Screen shades can also be bought or improvised (see page 214).*

› Information display

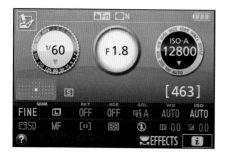

INFORMATION DISPLAY — ⌃
GRAPHIC FORMAT

The information display is central to using the Nikon D5500. To activate it, either:
– Half-press and release the shutter-release button (if you maintain pressure the information display will not appear); or
– Press **info** on the rear of the camera. This brings up a display showing the

selected exposure mode, the aperture, and shutter speed, and a range of other details.

This screen can be displayed in either of two formats. **Graphic** format, active by default, uses icons and pictures to illustrate the effects of various settings. **Classic** format presents the information traditionally, using text and numbers. You can also change the color scheme. Explore the options via the Setup menu (page 130).

INFORMATION DISPLAY — ⌄
CLASSIC FORMAT

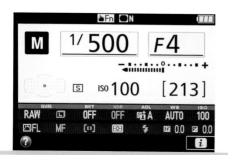

› Active information display

The information display described above is passive, i.e. it displays many settings but does not allow you to change them. To make changes possible, press ◄**B**► or tap **i** on the screen.

The screen changes, with the lower half now showing a range of items which you can adjust. (Not all of these are always available; it depends on exposure mode.) You can use the multi-selector to highlight the item you want, then press ⊙ or tap **OK OK** to reveal the range of options for that item. Alternatively, just tap the item you want.

Having revealed the options for a particular item, you can make a selection using the multi-selector or touch screen.

Note:
The term "active information display" is our own coinage. It is not used in Nikon's own manual, which instead refers clunkily to "placing the cursor in the information display".

GET ACTIVE ⌄
The active information display gives quick access to most important controls, such as exposure compensation.
28mm, 1/250 sec., f/5, ISO 320.

THE ACTIVE INFORMATION DISPLAY ⌄
WITH ISO SENSITIVITY HIGHLIGHTED

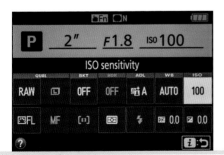

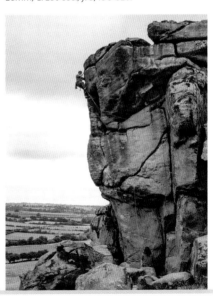

2

› Mode dial

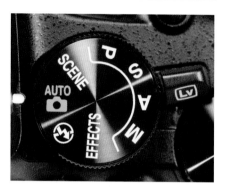

THE MODE DIAL ⌃

Exposure modes, selected from the mode dial, are fundamental to the camera's operation. The choice of exposure mode makes a significant difference to the amount of control you can—or can't—exercise. It has eight positions, split into four groups: Full Auto modes; User-control modes; Scene modes; and Effects. For a full run-down of these see under Exposure modes, page 38.

› Command dial

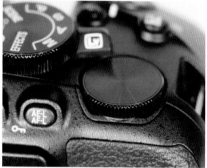

THE COMMAND DIAL ⌃

The command dial falls naturally under the right thumb when the camera is in shooting position. It is fundamental to the operation of the Nikon D5500, especially in the user-control modes.

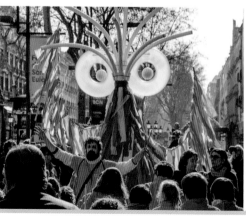

CROWD CONTROL »
One use of the command dial is for setting the aperture (see page 64).
70mm, 1/250 sec., f/8, ISO 200.

› Operating the command dial

The dial's function is flexible, varying according to the operating mode at the time. In Shutter-priority (**S**) or Manual (**M**) mode, rotating the command dial selects the shutter speed. In Aperture-priority (**A**) mode it selects the aperture. In Program (**P**) mode it engages flexible program, changing the combination of shutter speed and aperture. For descriptions of these modes see page 60.

The command dial is also used to choose between Scene or Effects modes when the mode dial is set to SCENE or EFFECTS. When shooting in **AUTO** and 🚫 modes, the dial has no direct effect.

› Multi-selector

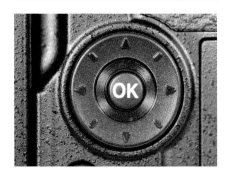

THE MULTI-SELECTOR　　　　　　　　　　**⌃**

The other principal control is the multi-selector. Its main use when shooting pictures is to select and change settings in the active information display; the ⓄⓀ button at its center is used to confirm settings. The multi-selector is also used for navigating through the menus.

The touch screen offers an alternative to the multi-selector for all of these operations.

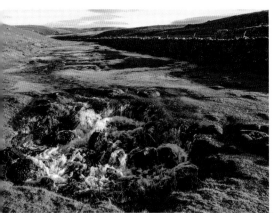

RUNNING WATER　　　　　　　　　**«**
Another use of the command dial is in setting shutter speed (see page 62).
22mm, 1/80 sec., f/16, ISO 200.

FUNCTIONS » BASIC CAMERA FUNCTIONS

2 › Touch screen

The D5500 is the first Nikon DSLR to offer a touch screen. For those used to more traditional cameras this may feel strange, although most of us are now very familiar with using such screens on smartphones and tablets.

The screen can be used to control most camera operations, from changing basic shooting settings to navigating the menus, and viewing the images you've shot. In some cases, using the screen may well be the quickest available method; for example, by swiping with a finger, you can scroll very quickly through a menu or through a series of playback images.

However, for other operations, such as changing shutter speed or aperture settings in user-control modes, it's much quicker to use the command dial. Like most touch screens, it's practically impossible to use it when wearing gloves.

The eye-sensor, just above the viewfinder, turns the information display off when you put your eye to the finder. This helps to avoid unintentional changes of settings if you touch the screen (e.g. with your nose). You can disable this sensor, if you wish, through the **Info Display Auto Off** section of the Setup menu (page 130).

If you prefer to interact with your camera in a more traditional way you can partially or completely disable the touch screen functions using **Touch controls** in the Setup menu (page 129).

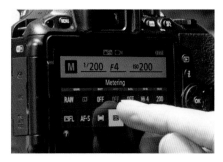

USING THE TOUCH SCREEN　　　　　　⌃

Tip

I find the ⎐ᵢ *button the most awkwardly placed on the camera, but there's no alternative, as Release mode is not among the options in the active information display.*

STAY SHARP　　　　　　　　　　　　　》
Release mode options (see following pages) include the use of a remote control or self-timer. Both minimize vibration for maximum sharpness.
100mm macro, 1/15 sec., f/8, ISO 200, tripod.

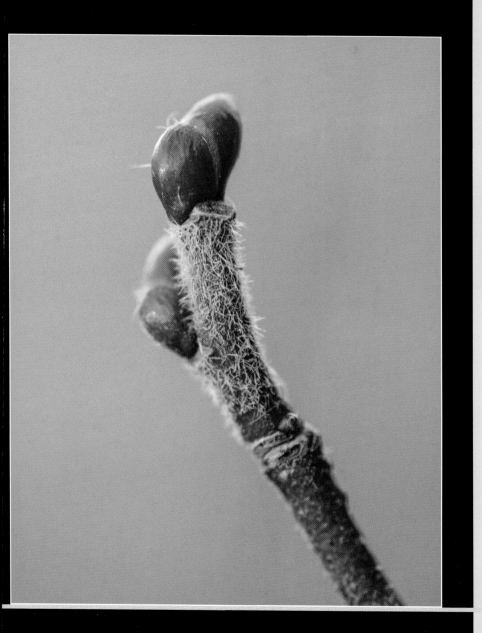

› Release mode

Release mode determines whether the camera takes a single picture or shoots continuously. It can also allow you to delay the shot or trigger the camera remotely. Seven possible release modes are available. The current mode is shown in the information display.

1) Press 🖳 to bring up a list of options (see the table opposite).

2) Release 🖳.

3) Tap the desired option, or highlight it

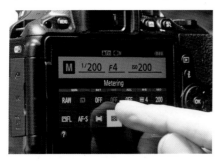

SETTING RELEASE MODE ⌃

using the multi-selector and press (OK) to make it active.

Another option, possibly quickest of all, is to hold down 🖳 and rotate the command dial to cycle through the options.

> *Note:*
> It's irritating that the camera doesn't remain in ☼ mode after you've used it once. I regularly take sequences of shots using the self-timer each time, and having to reset release mode repeatedly is infuriating. This could be fixed by a firmware upgrade (see page 132).

You can select Release modes in any Exposure mode, but whenever you switch to an Auto, Scene, or Effects mode, Release mode reverts to the default for that Exposure mode (usually [S]).

RELEASE MODE OPTIONS

Setting	Description
S Single Frame	The camera takes one shot each time the shutter release is fully depressed.
L Continuous L	The camera fires continuously while the shutter release is fully depressed. The maximum frame rate is 3 frames per second (fps).
H Continuous H	The camera fires continuously while the shutter release is fully depressed. The maximum frame rate is 5fps.
Q Quiet shutter release	Takes one shot. Mirror remains up and shutter does not re-cock until shutter-release button is released, making shooting quieter (but by no means silent).
Self-timer	Shot is taken at a set interval after pressing the release button. Default interval is 10 sec., 2 sec., 5 sec., or 20 sec. Can be set using Custom Setting c3. Up to 9 shots can be taken for each release. Camera resets to S after each release. See page 123.
Delayed remote	Requires ML-L3 remote control (page 214); shutter fires 2 sec. after remote is tripped. Camera resets to S if remote is not used within a certain time (set by Custom setting c4)
Quick response remote	Requires ML-L3 remote control; shutter fires immediately when remote is tripped. Camera resets to S if remote is not used within a certain time (set by Custom setting c4).

Images are held in the camera's internal memory ("buffer") until they can be written to the memory card. Usually you'll never notice any delay, but when you shoot images in a continuous burst you can fill up the buffer. How soon this happens depends on factors including image quality and size (see page 82), and the speed of the memory card (see page 216).

The maximum possible number of frames you can shoot in a burst at current settings is shown in the viewfinder at bottom right when you half-press the shutter release, e.g. **[r05]**. **(0)** means that the buffer is full; no more shots can be taken until enough data has been transferred to the memory card to free up buffer capacity. This normally only happens if you're shooting in a continuous release mode (⊑⊔ **L** or ⊑⊔ **H**), and results in a slow-down or a break in the rhythm of the shutter.

In theory you can shoot 100 shots continuously at 5fps, but this usually requires image quality to be set to **Basic**. At **Fine**, using a fast memory card, I've managed about 50 shots before observing a slowdown.

Buffer limits are much tighter when shooting RAW. If **NEF (RAW) recording** (page 84) is set to **14-bit**, the limit is about six shots before shooting speed slows

dramatically; if you change the setting to **12-bit** it goes up to about eight shots.

In practice, these buffer/burst limits are rarely a serious handicap. Even when shooting fast action, I very rarely feel the need to shoot more than a handful of frames in one burst. I do set **NEF (RAW) recording** to 12-bit for action shooting, but I'd still rather shoot RAW than JPEG.

Tip

Shooting lots of long, continuous bursts isn't necessarily the best way to capture the peak of the action—but it certainly does leave you with an awful lot of images to edit later.

CAPTURING ACTION »
Action shooting should be about timing, rather than firing off lots of shots indiscriminately. *35mm, 1/60 sec., f/8, ISO 1600, flash.*

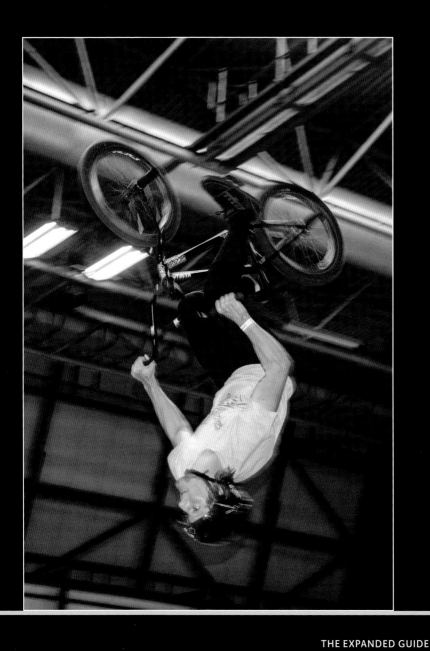

2 » EXPOSURE MODES

The choice of exposure mode makes a significant difference to the amount of control you can—or can't—exercise. The D5500 has a very wide choice of exposure modes, but they fall conveniently into three main groups: Full Auto modes, Scene modes, and User-control modes. There's also an EFFECTS position on the mode dial for more extreme or wacky results.

In Auto modes and Scene modes, most settings are controlled by the camera. These go beyond basic settings (shutter speed and aperture) to include options such as release mode, whether or not flash is used, and how the camera processes the shot. The difference is that Full Auto modes use compromise settings to cover most eventualities while Scene mode settings are tailored to particular scenarios. There is some scope to override the automatic choices—typically, you can change the ISO setting or turn off flash, for instance—but most settings are out of your hands.

User-control modes, by contrast, give you complete freedom to control virtually everything on the camera.

SMOKE AT SUNSET ⌄
Not all subjects fit neatly predefined categories. Is this a Landscape, Night Landscape, or a Sunset? You could try them all and see what works best. *300mm, 1/320 sec., f/5, ISO 200, tripod.*

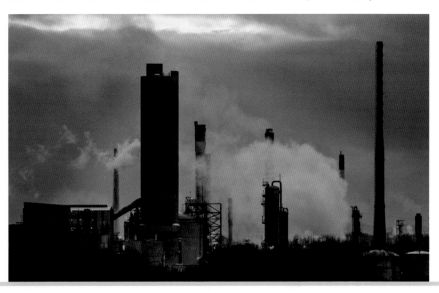

MODE GROUP	EXPOSURE MODE	
Full Auto modes	**AUTO** Auto	Leaves all decisions about
	Auto (flash off)	settings to the camera.
Scene modes (set mode dial to SCENE and use information display)	Portrait	Choose the Scene mode to suit the subject and the camera then employs appropriate settings.
	Landscape	
	Child	
	Sports	
	Close up	
	Night portrait	
	Night landscape	
	Party/indoor	
	Beach/snow	
	Sunset	
	Dusk/dawn	
	Pet portrait	
	Candlelight	
	Blossom	
	Autumn colors	
	Food	
Special Effects modes (set mode dial to EFFECTS and use information display or command dial)	Night Vision	Use for more extreme pictorial effects.
	VI Super Vivid	
	POP Pop	
	Photo Illustration	
	Toy Camera Effect	
	Miniature Effect	
	Selective Color	
	Silhouette	
	High key	
	Lo Low key	
User-control modes	**P** Program	Allows full control over the entire range of camera settings.
	S Shutter-priority	
	A Aperture-priority	
	M Manual	

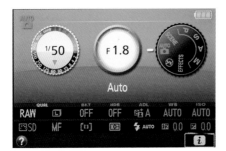

FULL AUTO MODE

In its manual, Nikon calls these "point-and-shoot" modes, which is probably a fair reflection of the way they're likely to be used. Left to itself like this, the camera is capable of getting acceptable shots under most conditions, but results may not always exactly match what you had in mind. This may be okay for snapshots, but limits creativity, and doesn't do justice to the D5500's full potential.

There's only one difference between the two Full Auto modes. In ⌖ Auto mode the built-in flash activates automatically if the camera determines light levels are too low (unless a separate accessory flashgun is attached and switched on, in which case this overrides the built-in unit). You can turn it off if you need to, but of course this just duplicates ⌖ Auto (flash off) mode.

In ⌖ the flash stays off, irrespective of light level. This is useful in situations where flash is banned or would be intrusive, or when you just want to begin to discover what the D5500 can do in low light.

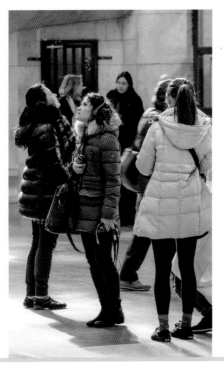

INDOOR LIGHTING
Auto (flash off) mode is useful when flash is banned, when it might be disruptive or annoying, or where it would destroy a mood.
155mm, 1/25sec., f/5.6, ISO 800.

Taking the picture

Basic picture taking is essentially the same in all Full Auto and Scene modes.

1) Select the mode by rotating the mode dial to the appropriate position; for scene modes, set it to SCENE and then use the information display and command dial/touch controls as described on page 32.

2) Frame the picture.

3) Half-depress the shutter-release button to activate focusing and exposure. Focus point(s) are displayed in the viewfinder, and shutter speed and aperture settings appear at the bottom of the viewfinder.

4) Fully depress the shutter release to take the picture.

Exposure warnings

In all modes, if the camera detects that light levels are too low or, more rarely, too high for an acceptable exposure, warnings will be displayed. The viewfinder display blinks, and in the information display you'll see a flashing question mark and a warning message. The camera will still take pictures, but results may well be unsatisfactory—for instance, if it's too dark, shots are likely to be underexposed.

A different warning appears when the camera thinks you should use flash because the shutter speed is too low, mainly in User-control modes (in 📷 and most Scene modes, the flash will pop up automatically). In the viewfinder you'll see a blinking ⚡ and question mark; in the information display, just the question mark. However, this warning can still appear even when the camera is on a tripod, when camera shake should not be an issue.

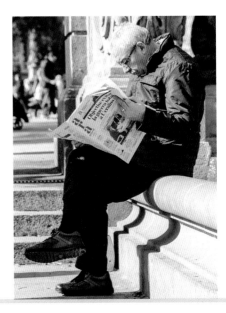

TAKE A BREAK »
Full Auto mode may be ideal when shots need to be grabbed quickly.
112mm, 1/250 sec., f/7.1, ISO 200.

2 › Scene modes

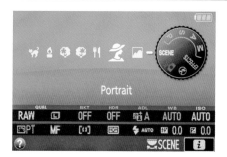

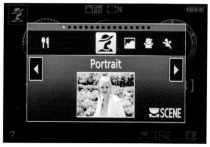

VIRTUAL MODE DIAL ⌃
A "virtual mode dial" appears briefly when you first set the mode dial to SCENE.

SETTING SCENE MODES IN THE ACTIVE INFORMATION DISPLAY ⌃

Scene modes are designed to tailor camera settings to specific subjects and conditions. Seasoned photographers may disdain them, as they take many decisions out of your hands. However, even the most experienced may find them handy as a quick way to set the camera for shooting a particular kind of image. If you're less experienced, you will find that Scene modes are a good way to discover how differently the camera can interpret the same subject as well as the full range of options offered by the D5500. The first step is to understand how the various Scene modes work and to be aware of the difference they can make in your images. With this in mind, it is interesting to shoot the same subject using different modes.

Scene modes control basic shooting parameters such as how the camera

focuses and how it sets shutter speed and aperture. They also determine how the image is processed by the camera (assuming you are shooting JPEG images, see page 82). For instance, Nikon Picture Controls (page 105) are predetermined. In 🪞 Portrait mode, for example, the camera applies a Portrait Picture Control, which gives natural color rendition and is particularly kind to skin tones. Most Scene modes also employ Auto White Balance (see page 77), but in a few cases the white balance setting is predetermined to suit specific subjects.

As you scroll through the modes, a thumbnail image gives an example of an appropriate subject for each mode, and the way it should turn out when this mode is used. The selection screen disappears after a few seconds; turn the command dial again when you need to reactivate it.

› ♟ Portrait

In Portrait mode the camera sets a relatively wide aperture to reduce depth of field (page 92), helping subjects stand out from their background. The camera also selects the focus point automatically, using Face Detection, although you can select other focusing options.

The flash automatically pops up if the camera determines light levels are too low, but can (and often should) be turned off via the active information display. If you attach a separate flashgun, this will override the built-in-flash—and the results are usually much better (see page 158).

PORTRAIT MODE ☒
Portrait mode restricts depth of field.
70mm, 1/50 sec., f/5.3, ISO 800.

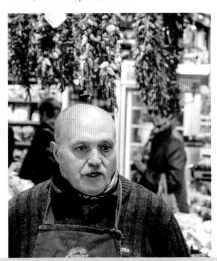

› ♟ Child

Child mode is broadly similar, but the camera tends to set higher shutter speeds, no doubt because children are less likely to sit still when required. JPEG processing is based on a Standard Picture Control rather than Portrait. This should give results that are more vivid overall but still with pleasing skin tones. There's absolutely no reason why you can't use Child mode when shooting adults too, particularly if they are active rather than sitting still; it works well for "candid" shots rather than posed ones. If you want to be really unobtrusive, be sure to turn the flash off.

CHILD MODE ☒
Child mode is tailored to more active subjects.
125mm, 1/250 sec., f/7.1, ISO 200.

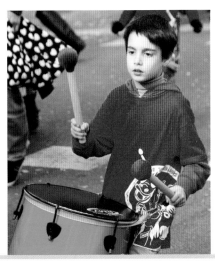

› ⚐ Night portrait

In most respects Night portrait mode is similar to regular Portrait mode, but when the ambient light is low it allows the camera to set a long shutter speed to allow an image of the background to register. For this reason, it's sometimes advisable to use a tripod or other solid camera support.

The built-in flash operates automatically. Again, red-eye reduction flash applies by default, creating an enforced shutter delay. Because the background should be brighter, this should mean results are less harsh than regular Portrait mode. Still, Flash mode can be changed via the active information display (see page 151), and an accessory flashgun will often give better results. JPEG processing is based on a Portrait Picture Control.

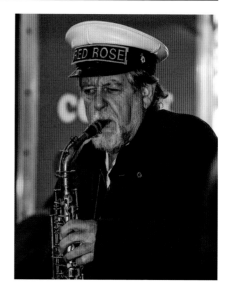

NIGHT PORTRAIT MODE ⌃
Night portrait mode blends ambient lighting with on-board flash.
100mm, 1/125 sec., f/5, ISO 1600.

› ⚑ Party/indoor

This mode is broadly similar, but does not allow such long exposures to be set— who wants to use a tripod at a party? JPEG processing is based on a Standard Picture Control.

PARTY/INDOOR MODE »
Party/indoor mode can be used outdoors, too.
18mm, 1/15 sec., f/4.5, ISO 1600.

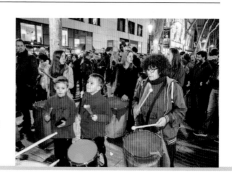

› ▲▲ Landscape

In Landscape mode, the camera sets a small aperture, aiming to maximize depth of field (page 92). The camera also selects the focus point(s) automatically, but you can override this choice if you wish.

Small apertures mean that shutter speeds can be on the slow side, so a tripod or other form of camera support is often advisable. A Landscape Picture Control is applied, to deliver vibrant colors. The built-in flash remains off; if you want to use fill-in flash (see page 146) to brighten the foreground, use an accessory flashgun or switch to another mode, such as Aperture-priority.

Tip

In Scene modes, Picture Controls and white balance are predetermined and can't be changed. However, if you shoot RAW (page 82) you can apply alternative settings in post-processing.

LANDSCAPE MODE ⨯
Landscape mode should ensure vibrant colors and good depth of field.
18mm, 1/60sec., f/11, ISO 100.

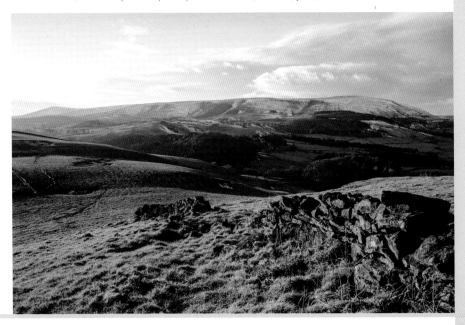

➤ 🎞 Night landscape

Night landscape mode allows long exposures to be used and therefore solid camera support, such as a tripod, is often required. The built-in flash remains off but an accessory flash can be used. Image processing, based on a Standard Picture Control, aims to reduce noise and preserve colors, including the varied colors of artificial light. When exposures exceed 1 second, Long exposure noise reduction applies, which creates a delay before another shot can be taken (see page 118).

The maximum exposure time is 30 sec.; if a longer time is required, use Manual (**M**) mode and set exposure to Bulb (see page 66).

NIGHT LANDSCAPE MODE ⌄
Night landscape mode allows long exposures. *18mm, 13 sec., f/11, ISO 200, beanbag.*

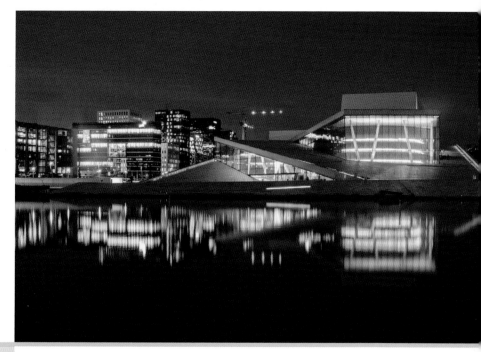

› ✖ Sports

Sports mode is suitable for shooting all manner of fast-moving subjects, not just sporting events. It's a logical choice for a lot of wildlife photography, for example, especially as there's no Wildlife mode. The camera seeks to set a fast shutter speed to freeze the movement. This is a reasonable approach to shooting action, but it isn't the only way to tackle it—see page 62 for more on this.

Using fast shutter speeds usually implies using a wide aperture and therefore shallow depth of field. The camera initially selects the central focus point (although you can override this). If it detects subject movement it will then track it using the remaining focus points. The flash remains off, so if you'd like some fill-in flash or mixed lighting (see page 146) you'll have to use a different mode; the obvious choice is Shutter-priority (see page 62). Alternatively, fit a separate flashgun. Sports photographers use flash a lot! A Standard Picture Control is applied.

SPORTS MODE　　　　　　　　　　❯❯
Sports mode is intended for rapid action.
200mm, 1/640sec., f/7.1, ISO 500.

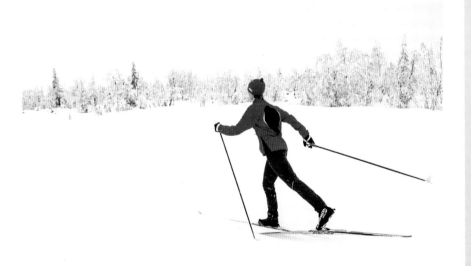

Close-up mode is, of course, intended for shooting at really close range. The camera sets a medium to small aperture to improve depth of field. This means shutter speeds can be low, so a tripod is often advisable to avoid camera shake. The built-in flash will activate automatically in low light, but it's a poor choice for close-up shots—a separate accessory flashgun is a far better bet. You can also turn the flash off via the active information display, or use 🍴 Food (see opposite).

The camera automatically selects the central focus point, but this can be overridden very simply, using the multi-selector (see page 90). This is a good thing, as focus is particularly critical in close-up shooting and the key part of the subject certainly won't always be in the center of the frame. A Standard Picture Control is applied.

CLOSE-UP MODE ❯❯
A tripod is often essential in close-up shooting.
42mm, 1/80 sec., f/6.3, ISO 400, tripod.

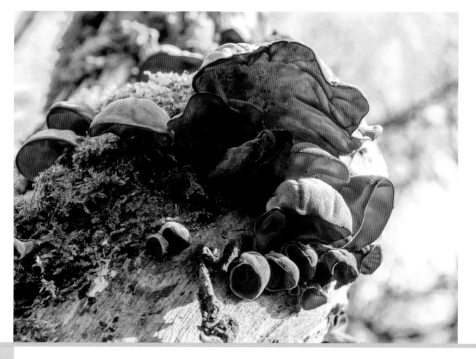

› ¶¶ Food

Food mode is unique among Scene modes
as the built-in flash does not operate
automatically but can be activated
manually with the ⚡ button. If the lighting
is too dim for a handheld shot, it is usually
best to use a separate flash or a tripod.
JPEG processing is based on a Standard
Picture Control.

FOOD MODE ⌄
Food mode can be handy for shooting other
close-up subjects without flash.
125mm, 1/100 sec., f/5.6, ISO 800.

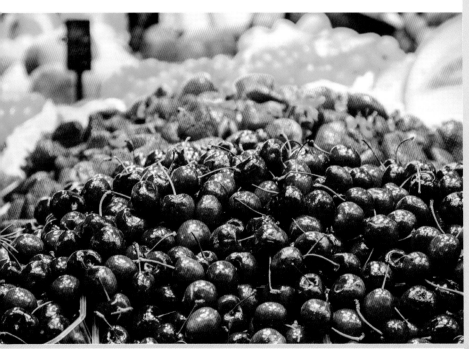

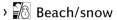
Beach and snow scenes all too often yield disappointing results—subjects are full of bright tones, yet pictures turn out relatively dark. The D5500 aims to counteract this, mainly by applying exposure compensation (see page 74). The built-in flash remains off, despite the fact that fill-in flash (see page 146) is often invaluable in strong lighting conditions; however, you can use an accessory flashgun. A Landscape Picture Control applies.

BEACH/SNOW MODE ≫
Beach/snow mode preserves a light, bright feel.
125mm, 1/160 sec., f/10, ISO 200.

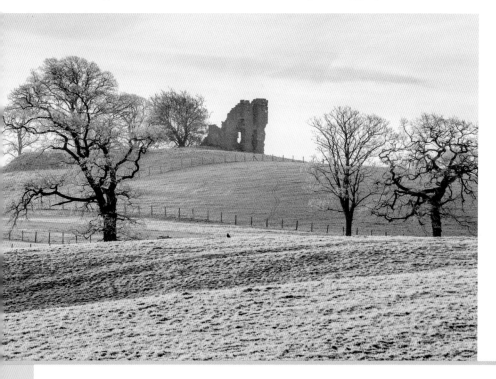

Sunset

Sunset mode has a number of similarities to Night landscape mode. The built-in flash remains off, although an accessory flash can be used to light the foreground; also, long exposure times are possible and so a tripod is recommended. However, white balance is predetermined to preserve the vivid tones of the sky. A Landscape Picture Control applies.

SUNSET MODE ⌄
Sunset mode is biased towards vivid colors in the sky.
32mm, 1/320 sec., f/11, ISO 160.

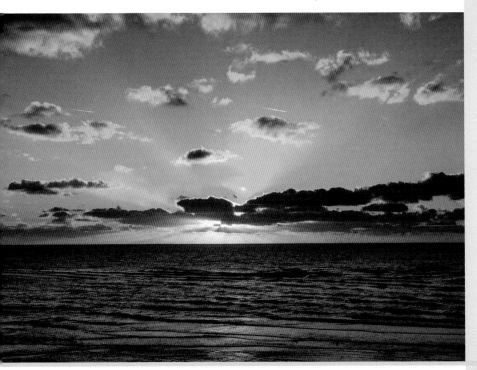

2 › ☀ Dusk/dawn

Dusk/dawn mode is also similar, but allows for the more muted colors and lower contrast before sunrise and after sunset; again white balance is preset rather than Auto. Flash remains off (although, as ever, an external flashgun can be used) and a tripod is recommended. A Landscape Picture Control applies.

DUSK/DAWN MODE ⌄
Dusk/dawn mode preserves the subtle hues and tones before sunrise and after sunset.
23mm, 2.5 sec., f/11, ISO 160, tripod.

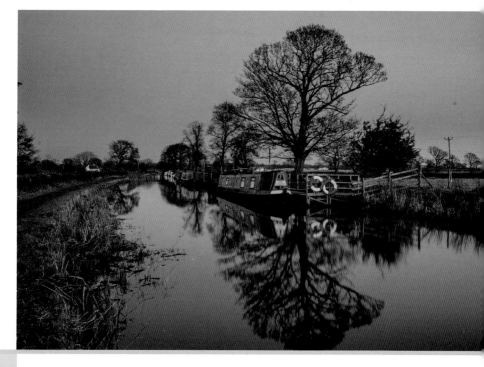

› 🐈 Pet portrait

Recommended for portraits of active pets, this mode is very similar in most respects to 🧒 Child, including the use of a Standard Picture Control. The built-in flash will fire automatically in low light but the AF-assist illuminator turns off, presumably to avoid disturbing the animal before the shot. The flash can be turned off via the active information display.

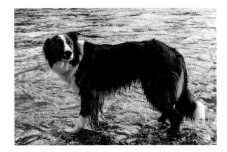

PET PORTRAIT MODE ⌃
It's someone else's pet, but pet portrait mode still works.
35mm, 1/100 sec., f/11, ISO 400.

› 🕯 Candlelight

Recommended for portraits and other subjects illuminated by candlelight. Because candlelight is quite weak, exposure times are usually long, a tripod is recommended, and portrait subjects will need to keep quite still. The built-in flash does not fire; it's possible to use an external flash but this generally defeats the object of shooting by candlelight. White balance is predetermined to allow for the very red hue of the candlelight. This mode could be used with other dim light sources but because the camera expects the light to be red, colors with other light sources may appear excessively cool. JPEG processing is based on a Standard Picture Control.

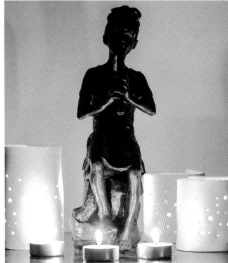

CANDLELIGHT MODE »
Candlelight mode does not completely neutralize the warm glow of the candlelight.
100mm macro, 1/10 sec., f/4.5, ISO 1000, tripod.

Use this mode for trees in blossom, fields of flowers, and similar subjects. Because the colors are intense, and blooms reflect a lot of light, detail is often lost in images of these subjects. In this mode, the D5500 employs Active D-Lighting (see page 104) to retain detail in these highlight areas. JPEG processing (based on a Landscape Picture Control) aims to keep colors vivid but not garish. The built-in flash remains off and, as usual, a tripod may be required in poor light.

BLOSSOM MODE ❯❯

Blossom mode preserves delicate tone and detail in flowers and similar subjects.
50mm, 1/60 sec., f/5, ISO 500.

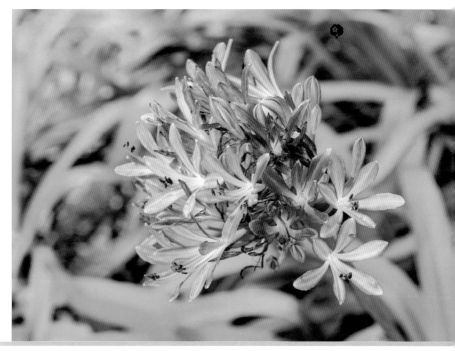

› ✿ Autumn colors

This mode is generally similar, but JPEG processing is based on a Vivid Picture Control. You could try it with other subjects where autumnal colors are paramount. Again, the built-in flash remains off and a tripod may be needed.

AUTUMN COLORS MODE ❯❯
Autumn colors mode favors vivid hues.
16mm, 1/15 sec., f/9, ISO 800, tripod.

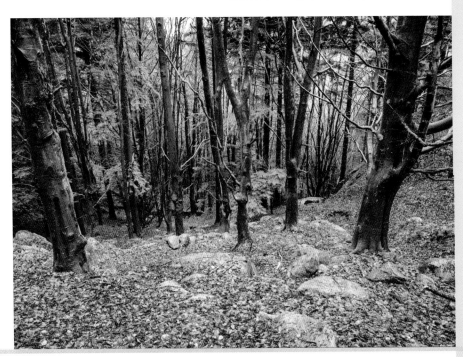

2 » SPECIAL EFFECTS

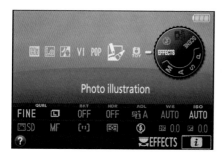

Photo illustration

Special Effects modes are Scene modes taken to extremes, producing various striking effects through a combination of shooting settings and image processing. They can be used in Live View or Movie mode. Some similar effects can also be applied through the Retouch menu.

Most of these modes always produce JPEG images. If Image Quality is set to RAW, the camera creates a JPEG image (Fine quality) instead. Exceptions are [icon], [Hi], and [Lo], which can deliver RAW images.

Live View gives a preview of the effect. For some modes, like [icon] Selective Color, this is essential. In Sketch, Toy Camera Effect, and Miniature Effect, shooting in Live View/Movie lets you modify the effect (press (OK) or tap OKOK to see options).

› Using special effects

1) Set the mode dial to EFFECTS.

2) Rotate the command dial to select the mode, referring to the information display, or use the touch screen. It's exactly like selecting Scene modes with the dial set to SCENE, and again using the command dial is quicker.

3) In Live View, press (OK) or tap [i] on screen to reveal shooting/processing options (if the current mode offers any). Choose from the options and press/tap again to continue.

› [icon] Night vision

This uses extreme high ISO settings (maximum ISO 102,400); produces monochrome images. Autofocus is available only in Live View/Movie shooting, and not always then: manual focus may be required. There are no options except for exposure compensation, and built-in flash not available.

> ### Tip
>
> *Night Vision allows handheld shooting in very low light—but it's mono-only, and quality is compromised. A tripod is usually a better bet.*

› VI Super vivid

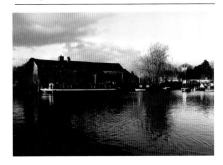

› Photo illustration

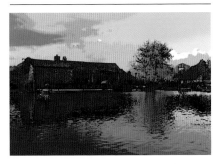

Super vivid boosts image saturation and contrast, well beyond a Vivid Picture Control, giving images an exaggerated quality. Super vivid mode works mainly by making deep colors even deeper. Images can appear dark and underexposed, rather than vivid and punchy. It works best with well-lit subjects without large, dark areas.

There are no fine-tuning options but you can preview the results in Live View.

› POP Pop

This also boosts saturation, but isn't as heavy on the contrast as Super Vivid. Still, expect images to look distinctly larger than life. There are no fine-tuning options but you can preview the results in Live View.

This simplifies colors and adds dark outlines where there are clear borders in the image. In Live View, press ⊕ or tap OK OK to access options for **Thickness**, which controls the appearance of outlines.

› Toy camera effect

The Nikon D5500 is a high-quality camera which can shoot fabulous images, but you can force it to mimic the effect of using a plastic-lensed "toy" camera (or applying popular Instagram filters) by creating a color cast and strong vignetting. (This surely counts as camera abuse, but there's no actual law against it!) The built-in flash is available. Live View options: **Vividness** and **Vignetting**.

› ⌗ Miniature effect

Mimics the fad for shooting images with extremely small and localized depth of field (see page 92), making real landscapes or city views look like miniature models. Movie clips play back at high speed. Live View options: use the multi-selector to reposition the in-focus zone.

› ✎ Selective color

Selects particular color(s); other hues are rendered in monochrome. Colors can only be selected in Live View (select the color under the focus point by pressing ▲ or tapping OK OK).

This selection remains active if you exit Live View and shoot using the viewfinder, but you lose the preview of the effect. The built-in flash is not available.

› ⌗ Silhouette

In this mode, exposure favors bright backgrounds, such as vivid skies, and foreground subjects record as silhouettes. Built-in flash is not available.

› Hi High key

This mode produces images filled with light tones, usually with no blacks or deep tones at all. Built-in flash is not available.

› Lo Low key

This creates deep, low-toned images. Built-in flash is not available.

LOW ISO »
As I was using a tripod anyway, I set the ISO to its lowest value to maximize dynamic range.
42mm, 1/15 sec., f/11, ISO 100, tripod.

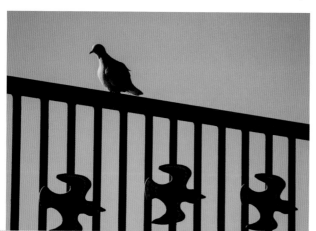

ON THE FENCE «
Silhouette mode can be very effective when used with the right subject.
180mm, 1/000 sec., f/8, ISO 200.

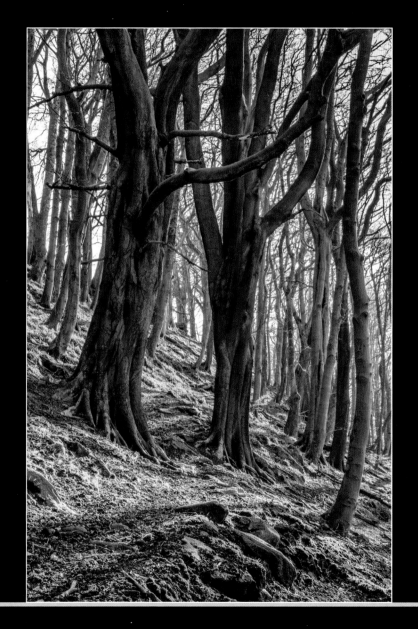

2 » USER-CONTROL MODES

The remaining four modes are traditional standards that will be familiar to experienced photographers. As well as allowing direct control over the basic settings of aperture and shutter speed (you can do this even in **P** mode by using flexible program), these modes give you free rein to employ controls like white balance (page 77), Active D-Lighting (page 104), and Nikon Picture Controls (page 105). They also allow manual selection of ISO rating (page 69).

These extra controls give you lots of ways to influence the look and feel of the image. You can also use the built-in flash at any time, but it will never pop up automatically.

› (P) Programmed auto

In (**P**) Programmed auto mode (often called Program for short) the camera sets a combination of shutter speed and aperture that will give correctly exposed results in most situations. Of course, this is also true of the Full Auto modes and Scene modes, but **P** mode allows you complete freedom to adjust other parameters too.

You can change things even more in **P** mode through options like flexible program (see below), exposure lock (page 75), and exposure compensation (page 74).

1) Rotate the mode dial to position **P**.

2) Half-depress the release button to activate focusing and exposure. The focus point(s) appear in the viewfinder image, and shutter speed and aperture settings at the bottom of the viewfinder.

3) Fully depress the shutter release to take the picture.

Flexible program

Without leaving **P** mode you can vary the combination of shutter speed and aperture by rotating the command dial to engage flexible program (also called program shift). This does not change the overall exposure. That is, it does not make the picture darker or lighter. What it does do is shift the combination of shutter speed and aperture, and you can see them change in the information display.

This is a very quick way to achieve practically the same direct control over aperture and/or shutter speed that you get in (**S**) Shutter-priority or (**A**) Aperture-priority modes. For example, you can swiftly choose a faster shutter speed to freeze action, or a smaller aperture to increase depth of field (page 92).

When flexible program is in effect the **P** indication in the information display (but not the viewfinder) changes to **P***.

PROGRAMMED AUTO »
This mode allows you to tailor camera settings to suit your own creative ideas.
50mm, 1/25 sec., f/5.6, ISO 1600.

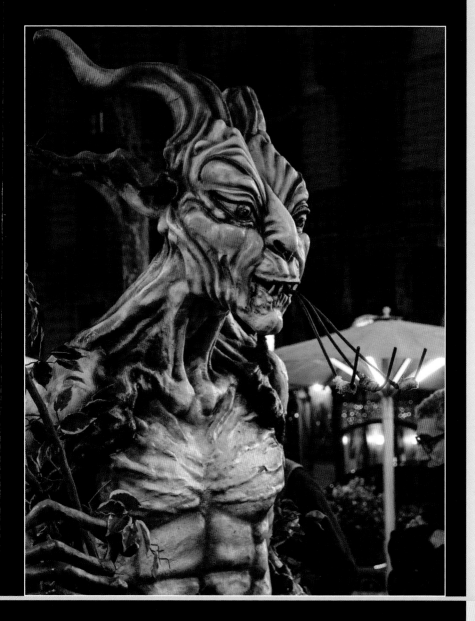

In Shutter-priority (**S**) mode, you control the shutter speed while the camera sets the aperture accordingly, to give correctly exposed results in most situations. You can set speeds between 30 sec. and 1/4000 sec. You can fine-tune exposure through exposure lock (page 75), exposure compensation (page 74), or exposure bracketing (page 76).

1) Rotate the mode dial to position **S**.

2) Half-depress the release button to activate focusing and exposure. Shutter speed and aperture settings appear in the viewfinder and information display.

3) Rotate the command dial to alter the shutter speed. As you change shutter speed, the aperture will adjust automatically. You can also tap ⟳ on screen then tap ◄ or ►, but using the command dial is much quicker.

4) Fully depress the shutter release to take the picture.

SHUTTER PRIORITY ⌄
A slow shutter speed, along with a panning movement, created a highly impressionistic result in this image of racing at the National Cycling Centre in Manchester.
14mm, 1/15 sec., f/7.1, ISO 200.

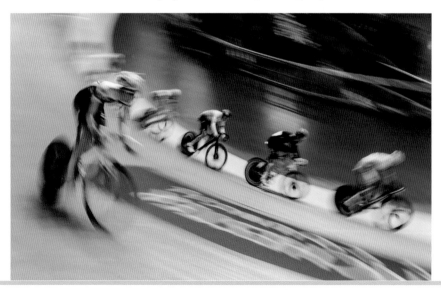

Significance of shutter speed

Shutter speed is significant mainly in relation to the way motion is recorded. Basically, high shutter speeds tend to freeze motion, while slower ones are more likely to record it with a degree of blur. This is relevant both to movement of your subject and to movement of the camera itself. Intentional camera movement and/or use of controlled blur, as in panning shots, can create very effective results—and is something that Sports mode does not cater for. Sports mode, although fine as far as it goes, does not give the direct control that you get in **S** mode.

On the other hand, unintentional movement, usually termed camera shake, can ruin a shot. Fast shutter speeds are just one way in which we can avoid or minimize the effects of camera shake.

Movement is not just a concern for sports and wildlife specialists. For example, it can be an issue in portraits (especially of children and animals). Even in "static" landscape photography, movement is often present, whether it's scudding clouds, running water, or foliage swaying in the breeze.

FREEZE FRAME »

A more orthodox approach to shooting cycle racing, with a fast shutter speed freezing all movement. The angle of lean and the rider's body language still give a sense of speed and dynamism.
116mm, 1/400 sec., f/4, ISO 800.

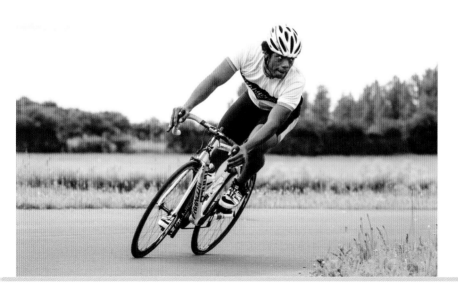

› (A) Aperture priority

In Aperture-priority (**A**) mode, you control the aperture while the camera sets an appropriate shutter speed to give correctly exposed results in most situations. Control of aperture is particularly useful for regulating depth of field (see page 92). The range of apertures you can choose from is limited by the lens that's fitted, not by the camera.

Fine-tuning of exposure is possible through exposure lock (page 75), exposure compensation (page 74), and possibly auto bracketing (page 76).

BUSKER ⌄
Here a long lens and a wide aperture combine to give shallow depth of field, softening the background and concentrating attention on the busker and cat.
200mm, 1/160 sec., f/4, ISO 200.

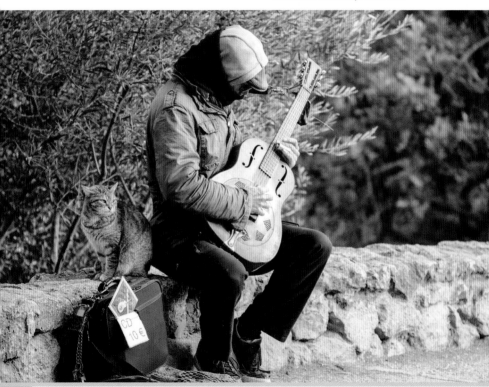

1) Rotate the mode dial to position **A**.

2) Half-depress the release button to activate focusing and exposure. The focus point(s) will be displayed in the viewfinder, and shutter speed and aperture settings will appear below the viewfinder image.

3) Rotate the command dial to alter the aperture. As you change the aperture, the shutter speed will adjust automatically. Alternatively, tap ◀▶ on screen then tap ◀ or ▶. Using the command dial is quicker.

4) Fully depress the shutter release to take the picture.

Significance of aperture

Aperture is principally significant as one of the key factors influencing depth of field. Depth of field describes the zone, in front of and behind the actual point of focus, in which objects appear to be sharp in the final image (see page 92).

What the numbers mean

Aperture numbers relate to the size of the opening within the lens which limits the amount of light passing through. It's a completely separate mechanism from the shutter, which is within the camera body.

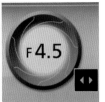 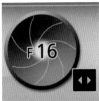

APERTURES ☆
Graphic representation of small and large apertures (although they should be written f/16 and f/4.5).

A wider aperture allows more light to pass even if the time (shutter speed) is the same.

Apertures aren't described by their physical size (e.g. 15mm) but as a fraction of the focal length of the lens. This number directly relates to the exposure setting whatever lens is in use.

Because they are fractions, aperture numbers should be (but often aren't) written as such, i.e. f/8 not f8. The information display (in Graphic mode) shows a graphic representation of the aperture, giving a useful reminder that f/4.5, for example, is large while f/16 is small.

In **M** mode, you control both shutter speed and aperture, giving you the ultimate in creative flexibility. Many experienced photographers use it constantly to retain complete control. If you haven't used Manual mode before, try it first when you're shooting without pressure of time and ideally when light conditions aren't changing every few seconds.

Shutter speeds can be set between 30 sec. and 1/4000 sec., as in Shutter-priority, but Manual mode offers two additional options: Bulb and Time (see below). These allow exposures of longer than 30 sec., which are useful for starry skies, fireworks displays, and much more.

To set shutter speed, rotate the command dial, as in Shutter-priority. To alter the aperture, hold ⊞ and rotate the command dial. The range of apertures that you can set is limited by the lens that's fitted.

You can also use the touch screen to set shutter speed and aperture. Tap ◀▶ below either the shutter speed or aperture indicator (if the display is in Graphic mode; tap the shutter speed/aperture indicator itself in Classic mode), then use ◀ / ▶ to change the setting. If necessary, touch ↩, then tap the other indicator to alter that setting too.

In this case the touch screen is painfully slow compared to using the command dial.

What's more, when using the dial you can change the shutter speed and aperture without taking the camera away from your eye.

B (Bulb)

Bulb appears in the viewfinder and information display. In Bulb mode, the shutter remains open as long as the shutter-release button is held down. However, holding it with your finger can cause camera shake and soon becomes tedious and uncomfortable. It's much better to use a remote control (see Accessories, page 214). Exposures of over 30 minutes are only possible in **B**.

T (Time)

Time appears in the information display. The viewfinder shows two dashes instead. Press and release the shutter button; the shutter remains open, either until you press the button again or until 30 minutes have elapsed.

STREET LIGHT »
Keen to retain detail both in brightly-sunlit areas and in the deepest shadows, I used manual mode and checked the histogram after the first shot.
125mm, 1/60 sec., f/8, ISO 100.

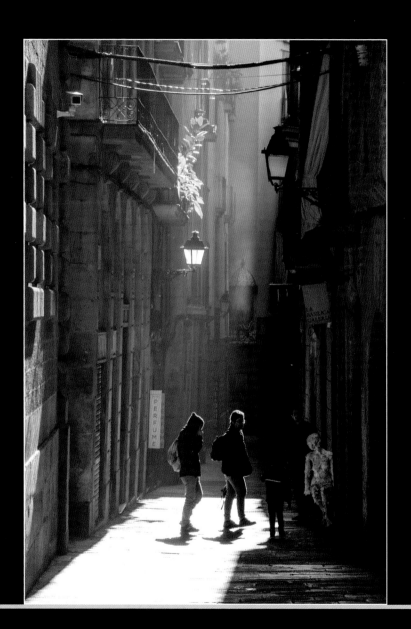

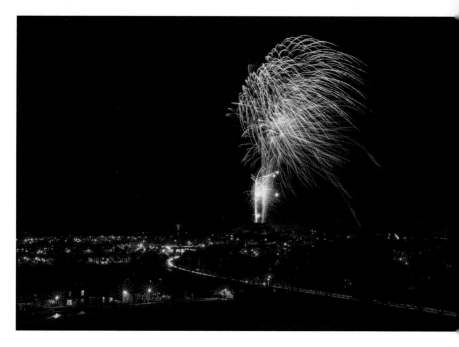

Using the Analog exposure displays

In Manual mode, an analog exposure display appears in the center of the viewfinder readouts and in the information display. This shows whether the photograph would be under- or overexposed at current settings. Adjust shutter speed, aperture, and/or ISO until the indicator aligns with the *0* mark in the center of the display; the exposure now matches the camera's recommendations. This exposure will generally be close to correct, but it is worth reviewing the image after taking a shot. If necessary, you can adjust the exposure for

FIREWORKS ⌃

Fireworks displays often require exposures longer than 30 sec., which are only possible in Manual mode.
35mm, 57 sec., f/22, ISO 100, tripod.

creative effect or to achieve a specific result. The Analog exposure display also appears in P, S, and A modes when you apply Exposure compensation (page 74).

» ISO SENSITIVITY SETTINGS

The ISO setting governs the camera's sensitivity to greater or lesser amounts of light. At higher ISO settings, less light is needed to capture an acceptable image. As well as accommodating lower light levels, higher ISOs are also useful when you need a small aperture for increased depth of field (see page 92), or a fast shutter speed to freeze rapid movement (see page 63).

Conversely, lower ISOs are useful in brighter conditions, and/or when you want to use wide apertures or slow shutter speeds. The D5500 offers ISO settings from 100 to 25,600. You can go even higher in ◙ Night Vision (page 56) mode, but quality really suffers.

Noise

Image noise appears as random speckles of varying brightness or color. It's most apparent in areas that should have an even tone, especially in the darker areas of the image. The D5500 generally produces clean images with low noise, but noise does increase noticeably at the higher ISO settings. At some point, especially if you're viewing on a large screen or making large prints, noise levels may exceed your tolerance—try a few shots and see for yourself.

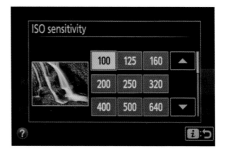

SELECTING ISO IN THE ACTIVE INFORMATION DISPLAY ⌃

Setting the ISO

The usual way to set the ISO is through the active information display:

1) Tap **ISO** or select it, and press ⊙⃝ to reveal a list of options.

2) Tap the required value, or use the multi-selector to highlight it, then press ⊙⃝.

You can also use **ISO sensitivity settings** in the Shooting menu, but this is slower.

There's a third option. You can assign the **Fn** button to ISO sensitivity in Custom setting f1 (see page 124); in fact, this is the default setting. At this setting, pressing **Fn** highlights **ISO** in the information display; keep it pressed and change the setting simply by rotating the command dial. This is the fastest way to change ISO settings, and for most people it's the best use of the **Fn** button.

Auto-ISO

By default, except in P, S, A, and M modes, the D5500 sets the ISO automatically. It's possible to change to a manual setting in most exposure modes (except 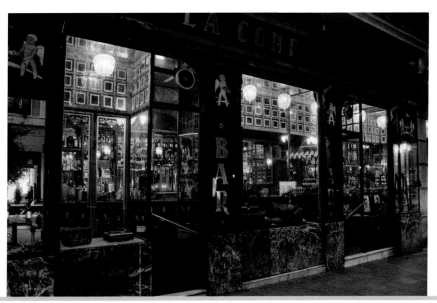, and). This new setting will continue to apply if you switch exposure modes. However, if you switch to **P, S, A**, or **M** mode and then back to a Scene or Effects mode, the camera reverts to Auto ISO. The D5500 only permanently "remembers" manual settings in **P, S, A**, or **M** modes.

Auto ISO sensitivity control

In **P, S, A**, or **M** modes, fully automatic ISO control is not available. You can visit **ISO sensitivity settings** in the Shooting menu and turn on **Auto ISO sensitivity control**, but it now means something different, becoming more of a failsafe. You still set the ISO manually, but Auto ISO sensitivity control allows the camera to deviate from your chosen ISO if this becomes necessary to maintain correct exposure. For example, if you are using Shutter-priority with a shutter speed of 1/1000 sec. and an ISO

NIGHT SHOPPING ⌄
Shooting handheld at night demanded a high ISO rating, but image quality holds up well. *18mm, 1/30 sec., f/5.6, ISO 1600.*

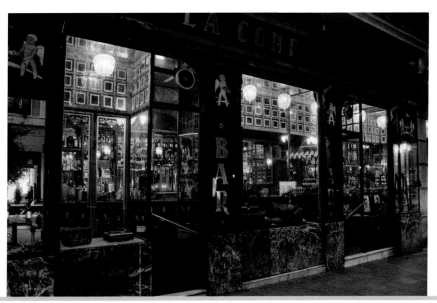

1/1000 sec. and an ISO setting of 100, light levels may not allow correct exposure within the aperture range available on the lens. The camera will adjust the ISO so it can achieve acceptable exposure at an available aperture.

The **Auto ISO sensitivity control** submenu has further options: **Maximum sensitivity** allows you to limit the maximum ISO which the camera can employ when applying Auto ISO sensitivity control. For instance, if you feel that image noise is unacceptable above ISO 3200, you can set this as the upper limit.

Minimum shutter speed allows you to set a shutter speed limit below which the camera will not go. This only applies in P

and A modes; in S and M modes you continue to set the shutter speed directly.

This submenu includes an **Auto** option; within this you can make a choice along a scale from **Slower** to **Faster**. If you err towards Faster, the camera will increase the ISO more quickly to maintain higher shutter speeds. The camera takes focal length into account; longer lenses require higher shutter speeds to avoid shake.

SMOOTH OPERATOR ⌄
I used a low ISO and a small aperture mainly to allow a slow shutter speed to smooth the flow of the water.
24mm, 0.8 sec., f/29, ISO 100, tripod.

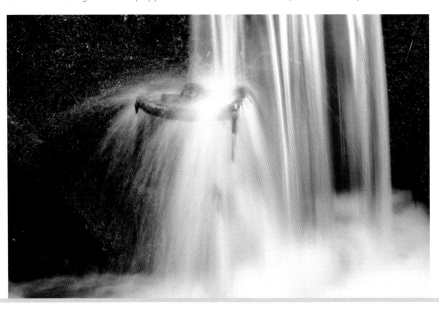

2 » METERING MODES

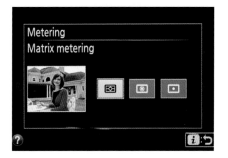

focuses—that's why it's called 3D. With other lenses, this distance information is not used and metering automatically reverts to a non-3D version.

Matrix metering is recommended for the vast majority of shooting and will nearly always produce excellent results.

SELECTING METERING MODE IN ⌃ THE ACTIVE INFORMATION DISPLAY

To ensure that images are correctly exposed, the camera must measure the light levels; this is known as exposure metering. The D5500 provides three different metering modes, which should cover any eventuality. Switch between them using the **Metering** item in the active information display (this is only possible in User-control modes; in other modes, matrix metering is automatically selected).

› 3D Color matrix metering

⊡ Using a 2016-pixel color sensor, 3D Color Matrix Metering II analyzes data on the brightness, color, and contrast of the scene. When a Type G or D Nikkor lens is fitted, the system also analyzes distance information based on where the camera

Tip

To be perfectly honest, I almost never use anything but matrix metering. My advice to anyone concerned about getting exposures right is to concentrate on mastering the histogram (page 102) first, as this is by the far the best tool for judging exposure. If matrix metering doesn't give the desired result, exposure compensation, exposure lock, and exposure bracketing (see the next few pages) are arguably all quicker and more intuitive tools than changing the metering method.

› Center-weighted metering

⊙ This is a very traditional form of metering. The camera meters from the entire frame, but gives greater weight (75%) to a central circle approximately ⅓in. (8mm) across. Center-weighted metering can be useful, for example, in portraiture, where the key subject usually occupies the central portion of the frame (although 🧍 Portrait mode sticks with matrix metering).

PORTRAIT ⨯
Center-weighted metering can be useful for portraits, especially when the background is much brighter (or darker).
42mm, 1/125 sec., f/8, ISO 800.

› Spot metering

● In this mode, the camera meters solely from a smaller area. If a CPU lens is fitted, this area centers on the current focus point. With a non-CPU lens, or if 🔲 Auto-area AF is in use, the metering point will be the center of the frame.

Spot metering may be useful where an important subject is very much darker or lighter than the background and you want to be sure it is correctly exposed (matrix metering is more likely to compromise between subject and background). For advanced users, spot metering can be an extremely powerful tool.

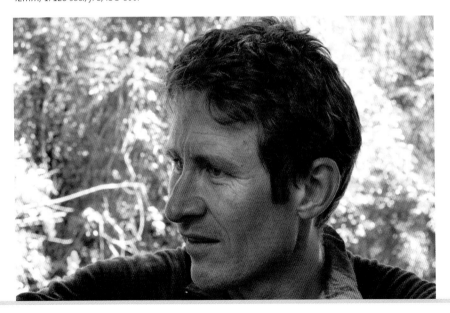

2 » EXPOSURE COMPENSATION

EXPOSURE COMPENSATION BUTTON ⌃

The D5500 will deliver accurate exposures under most conditions, but no camera is infallible. Nor can it read your mind or anticipate your creative ideas. Sometimes it needs a little help to get the result spot-on. Possible ways to do this include exposure compensation, exposure lock, and exposure bracketing (pages 74–76).

The principle is simple: to make the image lighter (to keep light tones looking light), increase exposure, i.e. use positive compensation. Conversely, to keep dark tones looking dark, use negative compensation. Remember you can check after shooting and have another go if necessary—the highlights display (page 103), and especially the histogram (page 102) are extremely helpful for this.

Exposure compensation is available in **P**, **S**, **A**, and Scene modes, plus 🌙 Night

Vision. In M mode, ⯐ controls the aperture, and you "compensate" instead by adjusting shutter speed, aperture, and/or ISO until the analog display shows a + or − value. In Auto and Effects modes (other than 🌙) exposure compensation is not available.

› Using exposure compensation

Exposure compensation can be set between −5 Ev and +5 Ev, although you'll rarely need these extremes. It can be applied in steps of ⅓ Ev (default) or ½ Ev, depending on the option selected for Custom setting b1. (This also dictates the steps used for general exposure control, e.g. aperture steps in **A** or **M** mode.)

1) Press ⯐ and rotate the command dial to set negative or positive compensation. Alternatively, tap ⯐ in the active information display, use the up/down arrows to set the value, then tap OK OK . Using the command dial is quicker, and you can do it with the camera at your eye. The chosen value is shown in the information display and in the viewfinder.

2) Release ⯐. ⯐ appears in the viewfinder.

3) Take the picture as usual. If possible, check that the result is satisfactory.

4) To reset exposure compensation, repeat step 1 until the value returns to *0.0*.

> **Note:**
> Don't forget step 4. Otherwise exposure compensation will apply to later shots which don't need it. It does not reset automatically, even when the camera is switched off.

› Exposure lock

For many people, exposure lock is the quickest and most intuitive way to fine-tune the camera's exposure setting. Unlike exposure compensation, it can be used in Effects modes. However, it's not available in Full Auto modes.

Exposure lock is useful in cases where very dark or light areas (especially light sources) within the frame can overinfluence exposure. It allows you to meter from a more average area, by pointing the camera in a different direction or stepping closer to the subject, then hold that exposure while re-framing the shot you want.

Using Exposure lock

1) Aim the camera in a different direction, avoiding especially dark or light areas.

2) Half-press the shutter-release button to take a meter reading, then press and hold *AE-L/AF-L* to lock the exposure value.

3) Keep pressing *AE-L/AF-L* as you reframe the image, then press the shutter-release button to shoot.

By default, *AE-L/AF-L* locks focus as well as exposure. This can be changed using Custom setting f2 (page 126).

> **Notes:**
> Nikon advises against using exposure lock when you're using matrix metering, but there's absolutely no reason not to do so if it helps you get the desired result.
>
> You can also opt to lock exposure simply by keeping the shutter-release button half-pressed. Use Custom setting c1 (page 122). Many people find this the most intuitive method of all.

2 › Exposure bracketing

Another quick and convenient way to secure a correctly exposed image is is to shoot several frames at varying exposures, and select the best one later; this is exposure bracketing. The D5500 allows you to bracket three exposures automatically, with up to 2 Ev between each one. Bracketing is only available in **P**, **S**, **A**, and **M** modes.

1) Ensure that Custom setting e2 is set to **AE bracketing** (this is the default setting).

2) In the active information display, tap **BKT** or highlight it and press ⊙, then use the multi-selector to select the exposure variation between shots in the sequence (from 0.3 Ev to 2 Ev, shown as **AE0.3** to **AE2.0**). You can also use the touch screen.

3) Press ⊙ or tap OK|OK again. *AE-BKT* is shown in the information display and *BKT* in the viewfinder.

4) Frame, focus, and shoot normally. The camera varies the exposure with each frame. In C_L or C_H release mode, the camera will pause at the end of the three-shot sequence.

5) To cancel bracketing and return to normal shooting, repeat step 2, and select **OFF**.

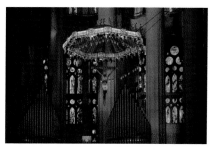
−1 Ev

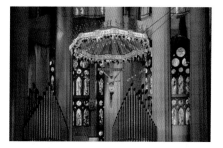
0 Ev

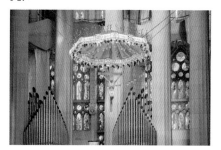
+1 Ev

125mm; 1/125, 1/60, 1/30 sec.; f/11, ISO 800.

» WHITE BALANCE

Tips

The D5500 offers alternative forms of bracketing; choose between them using Custom setting e2 (page 124). Instead of AE bracketing (as described here), you can bracket white balance or Active D-Lighting.

Exposure bracketing isn't ideal when shooting moving subjects, as the best exposure rarely coincides with the subject being in the best position. If possible, use other means to get the exposure right beforehand.

Light sources, natural and artificial, vary enormously in color. The human eye and brain are generally very good at compensating for this and seeing things in their "true" colors: we nearly always see grass as green, for instance. Digital cameras are also able to compensate for the varying colors of light and, used correctly, the D5500 can produce natural-looking colors under almost any conditions you'll ever encounter.

Automatic White Balance produces excellent results most of the time, especially outdoors. For finer control, or for creative effect, you can set the white balance (WB) yourself.

When shooting RAW, the in-camera white balance setting is less crucial, as it can readily be adjusted in post-processing. However, it's still helpful to get it right as it does affect how images look on the monitor in playback and review.

When shooting movies, when there's no RAW option, the right white balance setting can be vital, although using a Flat Picture Control (page 106) gives more room for maneuver.

There are two ways to set white balance (three if you count the **Fn** button, see page 124):

Using the active information display

1) In the active information display, tap the **WB** item to reveal a list of options. Or highlight it and press ⊙.

2) Tap the required setting, or use the multi-selector to highlight it then press ⊙.

Using the Shooting menu

This is a slower method but makes extra options available.

1) Press **MENU**, select **Shooting menu** and navigate to **White Balance**, or tap to select it.

> **Note:**
> If you use the active information display to select **Fluorescent**, the precise value will be whatever was last selected in the sub-menu under the Shooting menu. (The default is **4: Cool-white fluorescent**.)

2) In the list of options, tap the required setting, then tap OK OK . Or use the multi-selector to highlight the setting, then press ⊙.

3) If you press ▶ or tap **Adjust**, a graphical display appears. Using this, you can fine-tune the setting using the multi-selector, or by tapping a point within the display. Press ⊙ or tap OK OK to accept the new value.

4) If you select **Fluorescent** at step 2, a sub-menu appears from which you can select an appropriate type of fluorescent lamp (see the table below). You can fine-tune this setting even further by following step 3.

> ### *Tip*
> *If images consistently appear color-shifted on your computer screen, compensating by adjusting the camera's white balance is probably not the answer; the problem probably lies in the computer screen settings (see page 225).*

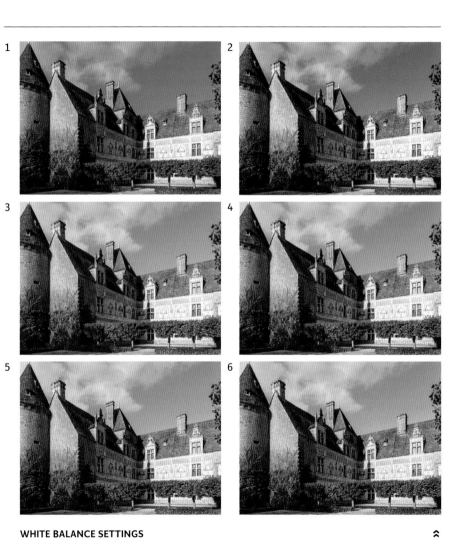

WHITE BALANCE SETTINGS
The effect of different white balance settings. Incandescent (**1**); Cool-white fluorescent (**2**); Direct sunlight (**3**); Flash (**4**); Cloudy (**5**); Shade (**6**).

ICON	MENU OPTION	COLOR TEMP.	DESCRIPTION
AUTO	AUTO	3500–8000	Camera sets white balance automatically, using information from imaging and metering sensors. Most accurate with Type G and D lenses.
☀	Incandescent	3000	Use in incandescent (tungsten) lighting, for instance, traditional household bulbs.

Fluorescent: Sub-menu offers seven options:

	MENU OPTION	COLOR TEMP.	DESCRIPTION
	1) Sodium-vapor lamps	2700	Use in sodium-vapor lighting, often used in sports venues.
	2) Warm-white fluorescent	3000	Use in warm-white fluorescent lighting.
☼	3) White fluorescent	3700	Use in white fluorescent lighting.
	4) Cool-white fluorescent	4200	Use in cool-white fluorescent lighting.
	5) Day white fluorescent	5000	Use in daylight white fluorescent lighting.
	6) Daylight fluorescent	6500	Use in daylight fluorescent lighting.
	7) High temp mercury-vapor	7200	Use in high color temperature lighting, e.g. mercury vapour lamps.

ICON	MENU OPTION	COLOR TEMP.	DESCRIPTION
☀	Direct sunlight	5200	Use for subjects in direct sunlight.
⚡	Flash	5400	Use with built-in flash or separate flashgun.
☁	Cloudy	6000	Use in daylight, under cloudy/overcast skies.
🏠	Shade	8000	Use on sunny days for subjects in shade.
PRE	Preset Manual	n/a	Derive white balance direct from subject or light source, or from an existing photo.

Notes:
Energy-saving bulbs, which have widely replaced traditional incandescent (tungsten) bulbs, are compact fluorescent units. Their color temperature varies but many in domestic use are rated around 2700°K, equivalent to Fluorescent setting **1 Sodium-vapor lamps.** In case of doubt, take test shots if possible, or allow for later adjustment by shooting RAW files.

The endpapers of this book are designed to serve as "gray cards", ideal for reference photos for these purposes.

› Preset manual white balance

You can set the white balance to precisely match any lighting conditions, by taking a reference photo of a neutral object. This may be vital when absolute color accuracy is required, as it sometimes is in professional work (e.g. when shooting fabrics or other products). However, it is a cumbersome procedure. See the Nikon manual for details—it takes four pages.

It's normally much easier to shoot RAW and tweak the white balance later; a reference photo can also be helpful for this when high precision is required.

» COLOR SPACE

Color spaces define the range (or *gamut*) of colors which can be recorded. The Nikon D5500 offers a choice between sRGB and Adobe RGB. The chosen color space will apply to all shots taken in all exposure modes. To select the color space, use the **Color space** item in the Shooting menu.

sRGB (the default setting) has a narrower gamut but images often appear brighter and more punchy. It's the standard color space on the Internet and in photo printing stores, for example, and is a safe choice for images that are likely to be used or printed straight off, with little or no post-processing.

Adobe RGB has a wider gamut and is commonly used in professional printing and reproduction. It's a better choice for images destined for professional applications or where significant post-processing is anticipated. However, images straight from the camera may look slightly dull.

SETTING COLOR SPACE IN THE ⌄
SHOOTING MENU

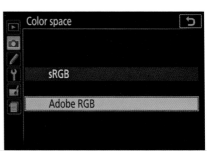

2 » IMAGE QUALITY

"Image quality" refers to the file format, or the way that image data is recorded. The D5500 can record two file formats: NEF (RAW) and JPEG. JPEG files undergo significant processing in-camera to produce files that should be usable right away (for instance, for immediate printing), without further processing on computer. However, this in-camera processing discards much of the information originally captured by the sensor.

NEF (RAW) files keep this data intact. This leaves much greater scope for processing later to achieve exactly the pictorial result you desire. This requires suitable software such as Adobe Lightroom (see Chapter 9, page 228). RAW or Camera RAW is a generic term for this kind of file; NEF is Nikon's specific RAW file format.

RAW files capture much more information than JPEGs and consequently produce larger file sizes. As a result, the camera takes longer to transfer them to the memory card. The maximum continuous shooting rate remains around 5fps, but the number of images you can shoot at this rate is limited. The exact number depends mainly on the write-speed of the memory card, but even with a fast (80Mb/s) card, I've found eight frames to be the limit before the shooting speed slows down drastically. If you want to catch a longer high-speed sequence, shoot JPEG, which allows you to shoot up to 100 images in one burst.

RAW files can be recorded at either **12-bit** or **14-bit** depth. Files at 14-bit depth capture four times more color information, but are larger, and so the camera takes longer to transfer them to the memory card. As a result, the maximum continuous shooting rate drops from 5fps to around 3fps. Even so, you can't shoot a long burst before the rate drops further.

The D5500 also allows you to capture two versions of the same image simultaneously, one NEF (RAW) and one JPEG. The JPEG serves for immediate needs while the RAW version can be processed later for the ultimate result.

It's often assumed that RAW is the "real" photographer's choice and JPEG is for the casual snapper, but it's not quite that clear-cut. You can get great results shooting JPEG (especially at **Fine** quality setting). However, there's less room to "fix" images

TO THE LIGHTHOUSE »
Shooting RAW gives much greater scope for post-processing, so you can get exactly the result you want.
12mm, 1/50 sec., f/16, ISO 320.

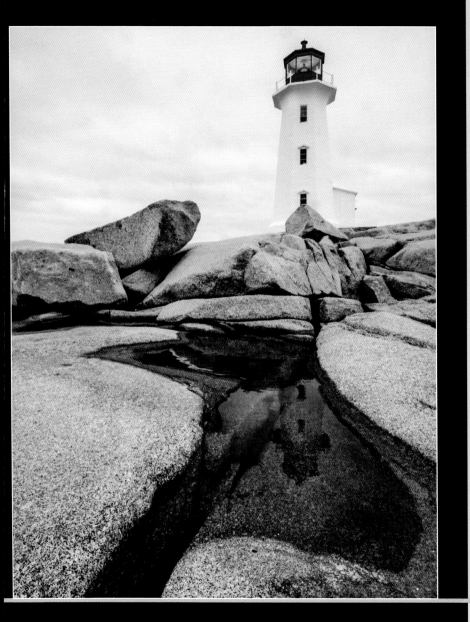

later. If you're serious about great results, shooting JPEG demands at least equal, if not greater care, especially in relation to exposure and white balance.

The majority of Effects modes (page 56) do not allow you to capture RAW files, because image processing is integral to these modes. When you use the Retouch menu (page 134), the end product is a JPEG image, as it is when you use HDR (high dynamic range) (page 108).

Tip

*If you've taken a shot in RAW but then wish you had a JPEG version, perhaps for immediate printing or to upload through Wi-Fi, you can create one using the **NEF (RAW) Processing** item in the Retouch menu (see page 135).*

IMAGE QUALITY OPTIONS

RAW	12-bit or 14-bit NEF (RAW) files are recorded for the ultimate quality and creative flexibility.
FINE	8-bit JPEG files are recorded with a compression ratio of approximately 1:4; should be suitable for prints of A3 size or even larger.
NORM	8-bit JPEG files are recorded with a compression ratio of approximately 1:8; should be suitable for modest-sized prints.
BASIC	8-bit JPEG files are recorded with a compression ratio of approximately 1:16, suitable for transmission by email or website use but not recommended for printing.
RAW + F **RAW + N** **RAW + B**	Two copies of the same image are recorded simultaneously, one NEF (RAW) and one JPEG (Fine, Normal, or Basic).

» IMAGE SIZE

› Setting image quality

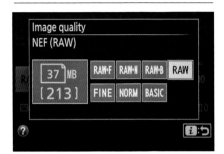

SETTING IMAGE QUALITY IN THE ⌃
ACTIVE INFORMATION DISPLAY

1) In the active information display,
tap **Qual** (Image quality) or highlight it
using the multi-selector then press ⓞⓚ
to bring up the list of options (see the
table opposite).

2) Tap the required setting. Alternatively,
highlight it and press ⓞⓚ.

Image quality can also be set via the
Shooting menu.

For JPEG files, the D5500 offers three
options for image size. **Large** is the
maximum available size from the D5500's
sensor, i.e. 6000 x 4000 pixels. **Medium** is
4496 x 3000 pixels, roughly equivalent to
a 13.5-megapixel camera. **Small** is 2992 x
2000 pixels, roughly equivalent to a six-
megapixel camera. Even **Small** size images
exceed the maximum resolution of an HD
TV, or almost any computer monitor, and
can yield reasonable prints up to at least
12 x 8 inches (30.4 x 20.3cm). **Medium**
exceeds the resolution of the new breed
of 4K TV sets.

RAW files are always recorded at the
maximum size.

› Setting image size

1) In the active information display, tap
Image size, or highlight it and press ⓞⓚ,
to show the list of options. (If **Image
quality** is set to RAW you will not be able
to select this item.)

2) Tap the required setting. Alternatively,
highlight it using the multi-selector then
press ⓞⓚ.

2 » FOCUSING

The multiplicity of focus-related options may appear confusing. The first essential is making sure that the camera focuses on the desired subject, or sometimes—especially in close-up photography—the right part of the subject. Other options determine whether the camera will refocus automatically if the subject moves, or only when you tell it to.

Where the camera focuses (what the subject is, if you like) is determined by the AF-area modes. *How* the camera focuses (e.g. once or continuously) is determined by the focus modes. This basic distinction is the same whether you're using the viewfinder, in Live View, or shooting movies. However the detailed options are different for Live View (page 96) and movies (page 176). This section only deals with viewfinder-based focusing.

Having focused at a certain distance, depth of field (page 92) then determines how much of the rest of the image will also be sharp.

› Focus modes

When the camera is in an Auto, Scene, or Effects mode, only two options are offered. Manual focus can always be selected, but the only autofocus option is **AF-A**. In **P**, **S**, **A**, or **M** mode four options are available.

1) In the active information display, tap the focus mode item (by default this reads **AF-A**) or select it and press ⊛.

2) From the available options, tap one or select it and press ⊛.

AF-A Auto servo AF
AF-A is the initial default setting for all exposure modes. AF-A means that the camera automatically switches between two autofocus modes—single-servo AF and continuous-servo AF (see below).

AF-S Single-servo AF
The camera focuses when the shutter release is pressed halfway. If you keep it half-pressed, focus remains locked on this point. The shutter cannot release to take a picture unless focus has been acquired (*focus priority*). AF-S is recommended for accurate focusing on static subjects.

FOCUS MODE SELECTION ☣

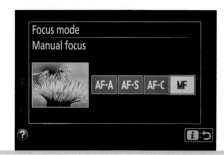

AF-C Continuous-servo AF

In this mode, recommended for moving subjects, the camera continues to seek focus as long as the shutter release is depressed; if the subject moves, the camera will refocus. The camera is able to take a picture even if it hasn't acquired perfect focus (*release priority*).

The D5500 employs predictive focus tracking; if the subject moves while AF-C is active, the camera analyzes the movement and attempts to predict where the subject will be when the shutter is released.

(M) Manual focus

With these sophisticated autofocus capabilities, manual focus might appear redundant, but many photographers still value the extra control and involvement. You might also want to use an old manual focus lens (but be careful—see page 188). There are also certain subjects and circumstances which can bamboozle even the best AF systems.

ON THE RIGHT TRACK ⌄
AF-C is recommended for moving subjects.
200mm, 1/1250 sec., f/8, ISO 400.

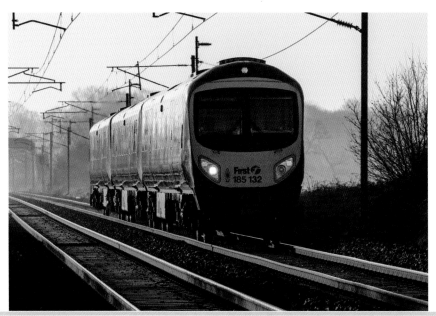

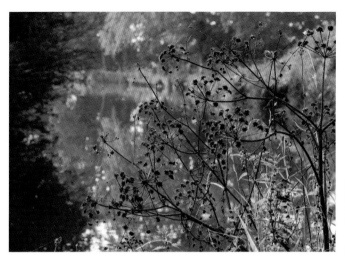

FLOWERS **《**
IN FOCUS
I focused manually
for precise control.
78mm, 1/320 sec.,
f/8, ISO 400.

Manual focusing is straightforward and hardly requires description: set the focus mode to **MF** and use the focusing ring on the lens to bring the subject into focus.

Focus confirmation
When using a lens that does not focus automatically with the D5500, you can still exploit the camera's AF technology via focus confirmation. Select an appropriate focus point, as if you were using autofocus. When the subject at that point is in focus, a green dot appears at far left in the viewfinder readouts.

In **P**, **S**, and **A** modes you can also use the exposure display as a focus guide or rangefinder; it indicates whether focus is slightly or significantly out, and whether the camera's focusing in front of or behind

the subject. It takes a little practice to interpret these readings and the rangefinder is off by default. Enable it in the Custom Setting menu (page 122).

AF-area modes
The D5500 has 39 focus points covering much of the frame; this area is indicated by a faint outline in the viewfinder. AF-area modes determine which of these the camera will use to focus on the desired subject. Select AF-area mode in the active information display.

Auto-area AF ▣
This mode makes focus point selection fully automatic; in other words, the camera decides what the intended subject is. With Type G or D lenses, the camera employs

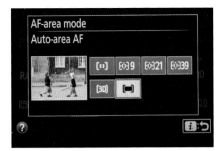

AF AREA MODE SELECTION ⌃

By default, the camera selects the focus point automatically (Auto-area AF), but you can change to manual selection in any shooting mode.

face-detection technology and, if a human face is detected, will prioritize it for focusing—which may or may not be what you want.

Single-point AF [ɪ]

In this mode, you select the focus area manually, using the multi-selector to move through the 39 focus points. The chosen point is illuminated in the viewfinder. This mode is best suited to relatively static subjects.

Dynamic-area AF [ɪ]

This mode is more complicated, as it has several sub-modes. These can only be selected when the AF mode is **AF-A** or **AF-C** (page 86).

In all sub-modes, you still select an initial focus point, as in Single-area AF. If the subject moves, the camera will then employ other focus points to maintain focus, but it's still trying to track the subject you selected.

The sub-mode options determine the number of focus points that will be employed for this: 9, 21, or the full 39 points. The final option is 3D tracking, which uses a wide range of information,

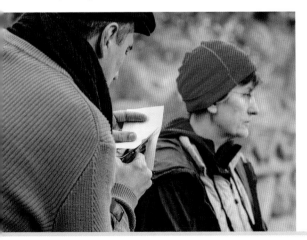

TO THE POINT «
The ability to select focus points is most helpful with off-center subjects, or if you want to focus on a very specific point—in this case, the hands of the silhouette artist.
92mm, 1/250 sec., f/4, ISO 200.

2

including subject colors, to track subjects that may be moving erratically.

Focus point selection

1) Ensure the camera is set to Single-point AF or Dynamic-area AF.

2) Half-depress the shutter release to activate autofocus.

3) Looking through the viewfinder, use the multi-selector to move the focus point to the desired position. Press **OK** to jump it directly to the center. (You can also employ the touch screen to select the focus point, if you choose **Focus point selection** in Custom setting f3: see page 127.)

4) Half-press the shutter-release button to focus at the selected point. If you want to use continuous AF, maintain the half-pressure. Press down fully to take a shot.

HUMAN PYRAMID ⏬
An example of the effect of shifting the focus point.
85 and 72mm, 1/1600 sec., f/5.6, ISO 400.

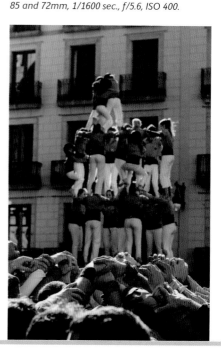

› Focus lock

Although the 39 focus points cover a wide area, they do not extend to the edges of the frame. To focus on a subject outside this area, you can use focus lock. It's very similar in principle to exposure lock (page 75). You shift the camera until the subject is within the area covered by the focus points, then select a focus point and focus on the subject in the normal way.

You then reframe the image to get the subject in the right place while keeping focus locked. In **AF-S** mode, lock focus by maintaining half-pressure on the shutter-release button, or by holding down **AE-L/AF-L**. In Continuous-Servo AF, *only* **AE-L/AF-L** can be used. Keep pressing the appropriate button to maintain focus lock for further shots.

AF-assist illuminator
A small lamp is available to help the camera focus in dim light. It works when the camera is in **AF-S** and the central focus is selected, or when **AF-A** is engaged. It then illuminates automatically when required. Obviously, its range is limited. It can be turned off using Custom setting a3, and is always off in some Scene modes.

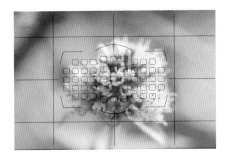

VIEWFINDER ⌃
The viewfinder displays the available focus areas.

> **Note:**
> At default settings, **AE-L/AF-L** locks exposure as well as focus, but you can change this using Custom setting f4.

AF-ASSIST ILLUMINATOR ⌄

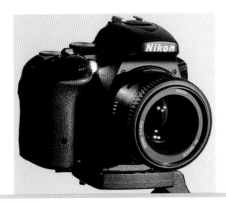

2 » DEPTH OF FIELD

We noted on page 65 that aperture is one of the key factors that determine depth of field. However, it's not the only factor—depth of field is a complex business. The other main factors relevant to depth of field are the focal length of the lens and the distance to the subject.

With long lenses and/or nearby subjects, depth of field may remain shallow even at small apertures. This is very evident in macro photography (see Chapter 5, page 164).

It's equally true that with wide-angle lenses, unless the subject is very close, it's not easy to get the sort of shallow depth of field which makes the subject really stand out from the background.

Sometimes a shallow depth of field is exactly what you want, as it makes the subject stand out against a soft background. For other images you may want to try and have everything sharp from front to back—this is the traditional (but not compulsory) approach in landscape photography, for instance.

DEPTH OF FIELD ≫
The combination of focal length, shooting distance, and aperture means that everything is sharp from front to back.
12mm, 1/160 sec., f/11, ISO 200.

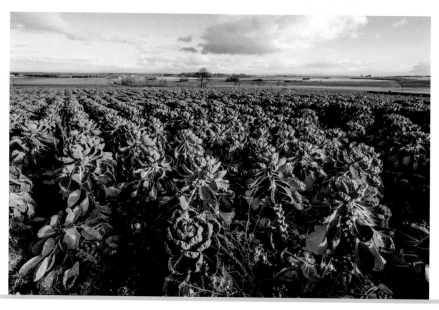

› Depth of field preview

When you look through the D5500's viewfinder, the lens is set at its widest aperture; if a smaller aperture is selected, the lens stops down at the moment the picture is actually taken. As a result, the viewfinder image may have much less depth of field than the final shot. Many DSLRs, but not the D5500, have a depth of field preview button—this stops the lens down to the selected aperture. However, this darkens the image and assessing sharpness isn't always easy.

In any case, there are alternatives. One is using Live View. When you enter Live View, the camera stops down to the currently set aperture. However, it doesn't immediately readjust if you change the aperture setting while in Live View. It will only reset the aperture when you take a picture, or if you exit and resume Live View.

You can also get a sense of depth of field by taking a test shot and reviewing it on the monitor. Both Live View and image review allow you to zoom in for a closer look. It can be a slow process but does give you a very good idea of what is (or isn't) going to appear sharp in the final image.

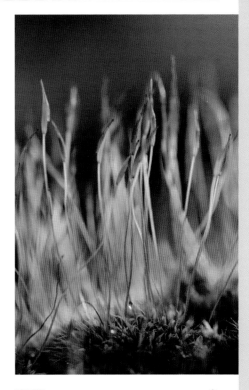

MOSS ⌃
At close range, especially in macro shooting, depth of field is inescapably narrow.
100mm macro, 1/125 sec., f/7, ISO 200, beanbag.

2 » LIVE VIEW

DSLRs like the D5500 are fundamentally designed around the viewfinder, and it still has many advantages for the majority of picture-taking. It's more intuitive and offers the sense of a direct connection to the subject. There's also much less risk of camera shake, and viewfinder-based autofocus is much faster. Live View is not much use in continuous release modes as the mirror stays up and the screen stays blank between shots. For both these reasons, the viewfinder is much better for shooting action.

However, to fully realize the high image quality of today's cameras, discerning shooters use tripods regularly—this dilutes the handling advantages of the viewfinder. Also, Live View focusing, though much slower than viewfinder-based AF, is extremely accurate, and touch technology makes it more intuitive. In Live View, the articulating screen facilitates shooting from awkward angles, when you can't use the viewfinder.

Live View is also the jumping-off point for shooting movies (Chapter 6, page 175), so familiarity with Live View is an advantage there as well.

› Using Live View

To activate Live View, pull back and release the **Lv** switch on top of the camera, by the mode dial. The mirror flips up, the viewfinder blacks out, and the LCD screen displays a continuous live preview of the scene. You can press the release button fully to take a picture, as in normal shooting, or opt for a touch shutter (see page 32). To exit Live View, pull and release **Lv** again.

Live View display options

A range of shooting information is displayed at the top and bottom of the screen, partly overlaying the image. Pressing **info** changes this information display, cycling through a series of screens as shown in the table opposite; press again to regain the starting screen.

LIVE VIEW ACTIVATION SWITCH ⏷

LIVE VIEW INFO	DETAILS
Show detailed photo indicators (default)	Information bars superimposed at the top and bottom of the screen.
Show movie indicators	Information for movie shooting superimposed; movie frame area also indicated (see page 175); pressing ◀█▶ brings up movie-related options.
Hide indicators	Screen clear of all information.
Framing grid	Grid lines appear, useful for critical framing.
Show basic photo indicators	Key shooting information shown at bottom of screen.

When Live View is active, pressing ◀█▶ superimposes a modified active information display on the screen, and you can select options in the usual way. Press ◀█▶ again, or press the shutter release, to hide this display. Most of the options are exactly the same as in normal shooting,

SHOW DETAILED PHOTO INDICATORS ⌄

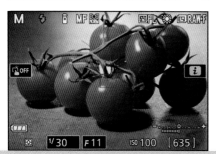

but the focusing choices are different (see page 96).

In Auto, Scene, and Effects modes, exposure control is fully automatic, except that exposure can be locked by pressing and holding *AE-L/AF-L*.

In P, S, and A modes, exposure control is much the same as in normal shooting. If you use exposure compensation, the brightness of the display changes to reflect this. However, this isn't a totally reliable preview of the final image.

In A mode, you can change the aperture setting but it doesn't actually take effect until you exit and re-enter Live View. In M mode you can't even change the setting without exiting Live View.

Focusing in Live View operates differently from normal shooting; because the mirror is locked up, the usual focusing sensor is unavailable. Instead, the camera reads focus information directly from the main image sensor. This is slower than normal AF operation—often very noticeably so—but very accurate. You can also zoom in the view, which helps in placing the focus point exactly where you want it. This aids manual focusing too.

Live View has its own set of autofocus options, with two AF modes and four AF-area modes.

FOCUSING IN LIVE VIEW
The focus area (red rectangle) can be positioned anywhere on screen, and you can also zoom in for greater precision.

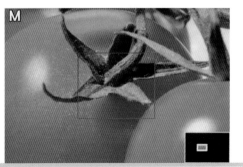

Live View AF modes

The AF-mode options are **Single-servo AF (AF-S)** and **Full-time servo AF (AF-F)**. AF-S corresponds to AF-S in normal shooting: the camera focuses when the shutter release is pressed halfway, and maintains that focus if you hold *AE-L/AF-L*.

AF-F corresponds roughly to AF-C in normal shooting. However, the camera continually seeks focus as long as Live View remains active. When you press the shutter-release button halfway, the focus will lock until you release the button or take a shot.

Selecting the Live View AF mode

1) In Live View, press ◂❚▸ to engage the active information display.

2) Use the Focus mode item to select between AF-S and AF-F (manual focus is also available).

3) Press ◂❚▸ again to return to Live View.

Live View AF-area mode

There are four Live View AF-area modes. They are different from those used in normal shooting (see the table opposite), although they perform the same basic function, i.e. determining how the focus point is selected. Again, selection is through the active information display—except in 🅰, 🚫, and 🎬, where AF-area mode is predetermined.

AF-AREA MODE	DESCRIPTION
🔲 **Face priority**	Uses face detection to identify people. Yellow border appears outlining faces. If multiple subjects are detected the camera focuses on the closest. Fixed in 📷, 🎆; default in most Scene modes.
🔲 **Wide-area**	Camera analyzes focus information from area (shown by red rectangle) approximately ⅛ width/height of the frame. Fixed in 🎥; default in 🏃, 🏞, 🐱, and most Effects modes.
🔲 **Normal area**	Camera analyzes focus information from a much smaller area, shown by red rectangle. Useful for precise focusing on small subjects. Default in 🌷 and 🍴.
🔲 **Subject tracking**	Camera follows selected subject as it moves within the frame. Not available in 🏔, 🌃, 🖌, and 🧸

› Using Live View AF

🔲 **Wide-area AF and** 🔲 **Normal area AF**
In these two modes, you can move the focus point (outlined in red) anywhere on the screen, using the multi-selector. Pressing 🔍 zooms the screen view—press repeatedly to zoom closer. Helpfully, the zoom centers on the focus point. This allows ultra-precise focus control, especially when shooting on a tripod— it's excellent for macro photography

(page 164). To return to a full-screen view, press 🆗.

Once the focus point is set, activate autofocus by half-pressing the shutter-release button. The red rectangle turns green when focus is achieved.

It's often easier and quicker to use the touch screen. Tap where you'd like to focus—this both positions the focus point and activates focus. The only limitation is that you can't zoom in or out with touch control; you still have to use 🔍 to zoom.

😀 Face-priority AF

When this mode is active, the camera automatically detects up to 35 faces and selects the closest. The selected face is outlined with a double yellow border. You can override this and focus on a different person by using the multi-selector to shift the focus point. Or tap that face on screen.

⊡ Subject tracking AF

When Subject tracking is selected, a white rectangle appears at the center of the screen. If necessary, move this to align with the desired subject; use the multi-selector, then press 🆗, or tap the subject. The camera "memorizes" the subject and the rectangle then turns green. It will now track the subject as it moves, and can even reacquire it if it briefly leaves the frame. To focus, press the shutter-release button halfway, or tap the subject again.

› Manual focus

Manual focus is engaged as in normal shooting (see page 88). The great advantage of Live View for manual focusing is that you can zoom in. When you press 🔍 the display zooms in to the focus area shown on screen. For static subjects, this is probably the most precise form of focusing available and it is my usual choice for macro shooting in particular.

› Touch shooting

Tap the 🖐OFF icon, at left in the Live View display, to enable or disable the touch shutter. If it's enabled, the camera will focus when you tap a subject on screen, then take the shot when you lift your finger off again. When it's disabled, use the shutter-release button to shoot as normal. While touch shooting will feel familiar to anyone coming from a smartphone or tablet, it's not clear that it has any other real advantages, and it can often lead to you taking unwanted shots.

FLOWER HEAD »
Normal area AF is the best choice for precision and accuracy, and well suited to the stringent focusing demands of close-up photography.

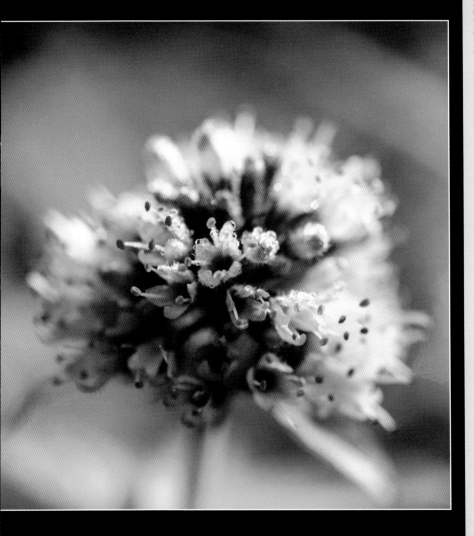

2 » PLAYBACK

The D5500's excellent screen makes playback pleasurable as well as informative. To display the most recent image, press ▶. If Image Review (see page 114) is **On**, images are also displayed automatically after shooting. In continuous release modes, Image review begins after the last image in a burst is captured; images appear in sequence.

Using the touch screen in playback is quick and intuitive, especially if you're used to doing the same on a smartphone or tablet. Even if you prefer not to use the touch screen when shooting, it's probably

PLAYBACK PAGES	SELECTION	DETAILS
File information	Always available	Displays large image, basic file info displayed at bottom of screen.
Overview	Enable from Playback menu	Displays small image, simplified histogram, summary information.
None (image only)	Enable from Playback menu	Displays large image with no other data.
Location data	Only appears when GPS location data was recorded during shooting (see page 132).	
Shooting data (three or four pages)	Enable from Setup menu	Fourth page appears if Copyright information is turned on (see page 128).
RGB histogram	Enable from Playback menu	See pages 102 and 114.
Highlights	Enable from Playback menu	See pages 103 and 114.

worth keeping it enabled for playback. This is one of the options in **Touch controls** in the Setup menu (page 112).

› Viewing other images

To view other images on the memory card, use the multi-selector or swipe the touch screen to scroll forward or back.

› Viewing photo information

A wide range of information about each image can be viewed on playback, using ▲/▼ to scroll through up to nine pages of information (you can't use the touch screen for this).

To determine which pages are visible, visit **Playback display options** in the Playback menu (see the table opposite). After checking/unchecking options, press ⓄⓀ or tap [OK] OK to confirm changes.

› Playback zoom

To assess sharpness, you can zoom in on a section of an image.

1) Press ⊕ (up to 10 times) to zoom the currently selected image, or use a "stretch" gesture (dragging two fingers apart) on the screen. A small navigation window appears briefly, with a yellow outline indicating the visible area.

2) Use the multi-selector or drag with a finger to view other areas of the image.

3) Rotate the command dial to see other images at the same magnification.

4) To return to full-frame view, press ⓄⓀ.

› Viewing images as thumbnails

Press ⊖██ or use a "pinch" gesture to display 4 images; repeat to see 12 or 80. The selected image is outlined in yellow.

Tip

High magnification (10 presses on ⊕) shows a pixelated image of debatable value—even the best images no longer look sharp. Eight presses is enough for critical viewing. The bar at the bottom of the navigation window turns green at this zoom level.

VIEWING IMAGES AS THUMBNAILS ⌄

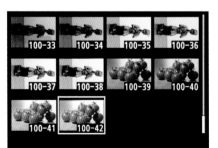

› Calendar view

Calendar View displays images grouped by the date on which they were taken. With 72 images displayed, press ⊖⊞ or "pinch" again to reach the first calendar page (date view), with the most recent date highlighted, and pictures from that date in a strip on the right (the thumbnail list). Use the multi-selector or tap to select other dates. Press ⊖⊞ again to enter the thumbnail list so you can scroll through pictures from the selected date; press ⊕ or tap for a larger preview of the selected image.

CALENDAR VIEW   ⌄

› Deleting images

To delete the current image, or the selected image in thumbnail view, press 🗑. A confirmation dialog appears. To proceed, press 🗑 again; to cancel, press ▶.

In Calendar View you can also delete all images taken on a selected date. Highlight

that date in Date View, then press 🗑; when the confirmation dialog appears, press 🗑 again to delete or ▶ to cancel.

› Protecting images

To protect the current image, press **AE-L/AF-L**. To remove protection, press again. Protected images can't be deleted as above, but still will be deleted when the memory card is formatted.

› Histogram displays

The histogram is a kind of graph showing the distribution of dark and light tones in an image. For assessing whether images are correctly exposed, it's much more objective than examining the playback image itself—especially in bright conditions, when it's hard to see the screen image clearly.

RGB HISTOGRAM DISPLAY   ⌄
This histogram shows a good spread of tones and there are no spikes at the left or right extremes, which would indicate loss of detail (clipping) in shadows or highlights.

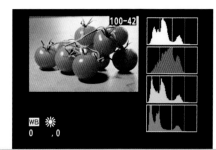

The overview page shows a single histogram; checking **RGB histogram** under **Playback display options** in the Playback menu gives access to a display showing individual histograms for the three color channels (red, green, and blue). The histogram display is a core feature of image playback and usually the page I view first.

When you shoot RAW, the Histogram (and Highlights) displays are based on the JPEG preview embedded with each RAW file. This means they aren't a foolproof guide to the potential for recovering highlight or shadow detail in that RAW file. This is particularly true when using "punchy" Picture Controls such as Vivid or Landscape, when JPEG processing discards more of the RAW data.

› Highlights display

The Nikon D5500 can also display a flashing warning over areas of the image with "clipped" highlights, i.e. they're completely white, with no detail recorded. This is another useful and objective method of checking exposure.

INTO THE SUN   ⌄
I wanted the image to have as much luminosity as possible, but knew that if I overexposed even slightly the bright background could easily blow out, so I checked the highlight display after the first shot.
15mm, 1/320 sec., f/10, ISO 100.

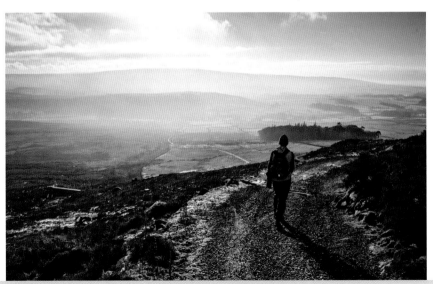

There are two main kinds of in-camera image adjustment and enhancement. First, certain settings can be applied before shooting an image; these are covered in this section. Second, you can create retouched copies of existing images—do this via the Retouch menu (see page 134).

Many of the controls that we've already considered have obvious and direct effects in the final image: aperture, shutter speed, ISO, white balance, and many more. Two other important ways to control the qualities of the image are Nikon Picture Controls and Active D-Lighting. These settings directly affect JPEG images, but shouldn't be ignored when shooting RAW, as we'll see.

› Active D-Lighting

Active D-Lighting enhances the D5500's ability to handle scenes with a wide range of brightness (dynamic range). Essentially, it reduces the overall exposure in order to capture more detail in the brightest areas, while mid-tones and shadows are

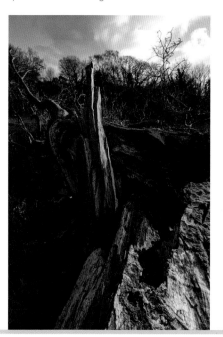
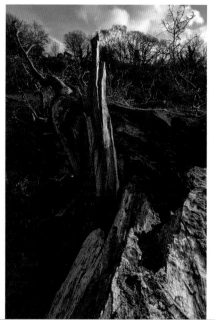

lightened as the camera processes the image. Don't confuse it with D-Lighting (page 137), a Retouch menu option.

1) In the active information display, tap **ADL** or select it and press (OK). Or select **Active D-Lighting** in the Shooting menu.

2) Select from the options to determine the strength of the effect (the default setting is **Auto**).

ADL bracketing
You can set the camera to take two shots, one with Active D-Lighting off and one with it on, using the current setting (see above).

1) Set Custom setting e2 to ADL bracketing.

2) In the active information display, tap **BKT** or highlight it and press (OK).

3) Tap **ADL** or select it and press (OK).

TREE STUMP «
Active D-Lighting comparison: Off (left) and Extra High (right). The shot with ADL has much better detail in the shadows, but also copes well with the bright clouds due to the lower overall exposure.
12mm, 1/60 and 1/125 sec., f/11, ISO 125.

› Picture controls

Picture Controls determine how the camera processes JPEG images. They also affect the preview image associated with each RAW file, on which Histogram and Highlights displays are based. Picture Controls also affect the appearance of the Live View preview image.

There are seven pre-loaded Picture Controls: **Standard**, **Neutral**, **Vivid**, **Monochrome**, **Portrait**, **Landscape**, and **Flat**. These are mostly fairly self-explanatory. Portrait, for example, uses moderate settings for contrast, sharpening and saturation, aiming to deliver natural colors and flattering skin tones. Landscape produces higher contrast and saturation for more vibrant, punchy images. The Flat Picture Control deserves additional explanation (see below).

COLOR COMPARISON ≈
Vivid (left) and Neutral (right) Picture Controls applied to the same subject.
55mm, 1/60 sec., f/8, ISO 400.

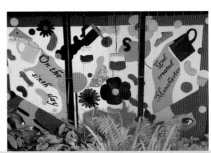

From here on, alternate shots will be taken with and without Active D-Lighting, until bracketing is canceled. To cancel, repeat steps 2 and 3, selecting **OFF** in step 3.

Selecting Picture Controls

1) In the active information display, tap **Set Picture Control** or highlight it and press 🆗. Alternatively, in the Shooting menu, select **Set Picture Control**.

2) Tap the required Picture Control, or highlight it using the multi-selector, then press 🆗.

This Picture Control will now apply to all images taken in **P**, **S**, **A**, or **M** modes. Scene/Effects modes continue to apply their preset Picture Controls.

Modifying Picture Controls

In the Shooting menu, select **Set Picture Control**, highlight the required Picture

---

PICTURE CONTROL SELECTION IN THE ≽
ACTIVE INFORMATION DISPLAY

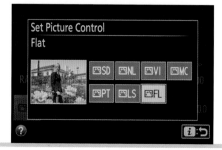

Control, then press ▶. Select **Quick Adjust** or one of the specific parameters. Use ▶ or ◀ to change the values. When all parameters are as required, press 🆗 or tap ⬛OK OK . Modified values are retained until you modify that Picture Control again.

Custom Picture Controls

You can create up to nine additional Picture Controls, either in-camera or using the Picture Control Utility included with Nikon View NX2. For further details see Picture Control Utility's Help pages.

To create Custom Picture Controls in-camera, select **Manage Picture Control** from the Photo Shooting menu. Select **Save/edit** and press ▶. Highlight an existing Picture Control and press ▶ again. Edit the Picture Control as described above under Modifying Picture Controls. When satisfied, press 🆗 or tap ⬛OK OK .

By default, the new version takes its name from the existing Picture Control on which it is based, plus a two-digit number (e.g. "VIVID-02"). You can give it a new name (up to 19 characters long) using the touch screen or multi-selector to enter text. (For more on text entry see page 128.) Finally, press 🆗 or tap ⬛OK OK to save the new Picture Control.

Flat Picture Control

The Flat Picture Control produces images which appear very subdued, with low contrast and saturation and no in-camera

---

sharpening. It's aimed mainly at movie-makers who intend to work on the color, contrast, and so on, of their footage later ("grading"). It's designed to preserve as much data as possible, giving maximum headroom for later adjustments and allowing movie shooters some of the flexibility and control that stills photographers gain by shooting RAW.

It can have value for stills photographers too, at least when shooting RAW. As mentioned above, the Histogram and Highlights displays are based on the JPEG preview embedded with each RAW file. These displays will give a more accurate guide to the potential of the RAW file when you use a Flat Picture Control.

RIVER RUNS THROUGH IT ⊗
This is an obvious case for using a Landscape Picture Control.
35mm, 0.4 sec., f/11, ISO 100, tripod.

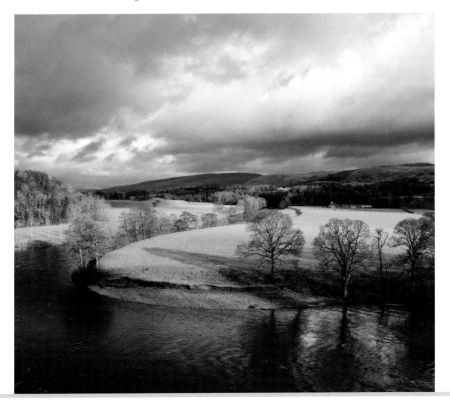

"Contrast", "dynamic range", "tonal range": all refer to the range of brightness between the brightest and darkest areas of a scene. Our eyes adjust continuously, allowing us to see detail in both bright areas and deep shade. By comparison, even the best cameras can fall short, losing detail ("clipping") in shadows, highlights, or even both.

Possible remedies include shooting RAW, using Active D-Lighting for JPEG images, or fill-in flash (page 146). Even so, sometimes it's impossible to capture the entire brightness range of a scene in a single exposure. The histogram (page 102) and highlights (page 103) displays help identify such cases.

One solution is to shoot several exposures and then combine the results. The D5500 can automate this, creating a high-dynamic-range JPEG image by merging two separate shots, with one exposure biased towards the shadows and one towards the highlights. HDR can be combined with Active D-Lighting for even greater range.

Because HDR merges two exposures, it can give odd results with moving subjects.

1) Select HDR in the active information display. It is only available when Image Quality is set to JPEG, not RAW or RAW+JPEG.

2) Tap an option, or select it and press (OK), to choose the strength of the effect. Auto allows the camera to determine this automatically, or you can select **Low**, **Normal**, **High**, or **Extra High**.

3) Shoot as normal. Because two exposures are made, it's a good idea to use a tripod or some other solid support. Results with moving subjects may appear odd; try Active D-Lighting instead.

4) The camera automatically shoots two images in quick succession. It then takes a few seconds to combine them and display the results. During this interval **Job Hdr** appears in the viewfinder and you can't take further shots.

5) HDR shooting is automatically canceled. To shoot more HDR images, repeat the process from step 1.

HIGH DYNAMIC RANGE »
An HDR image and two (simulated) source frames (insets): HDR strength was High.
"Source" images: 12mm, 1/20 and 1/80 sec., f/11, ISO 100.

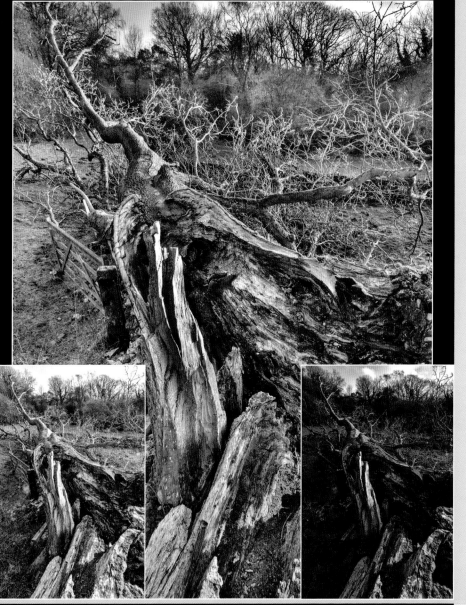

3 MENUS

The options in the preceding chapter are just the beginning. The menus offer many more ways to customize the D5500 to suit your needs. There are six main menus: **Playback**, **Shooting**, **Custom Setting**, **Setup**, **Retouch**, and **My Menu/Recent Settings**.

The **Playback menu**, outlined in blue, covers functions related to playback, like viewing and deleting images. The **Shooting menu**, outlined in green, is used to control shooting settings, such as ISO, white balance, or Active D-Lighting. Many of these, as we've already seen, can be accessed by other means. The **Custom Setting menu**, outlined in red, lets you fine-tune and personalize many aspects of the camera's operation. The **Setup menu**, outlined in orange, governs a range of functions such as LCD brightness, plus others that you may need to change only rarely, such as language and time settings. The **Retouch menu**, outlined in purple, lets you create modified copies of images on the memory card. Finally **My Menu** is outlined in gray; it is a handy place to store items from the other menus that you find yourself using regularly. Alternatively, it can become a **Recent Settings** menu.

Navigating the menus—multi-selector
The general procedure for navigating and selecting items from the menus is the same throughout:

1) To display the main menu screen, press **MENU**.

2) Use ▲ / ▼ to highlight the different menu items in the strip on the left. To enter the desired menu, press ▶.

3) Use ▲ / ▼ to highlight specific menu items. To select an item, press ▶. In most cases this will take you to a further set of options.

4) Use ▲ / ▼ to choose the desired setting. To select, press ▶ or (OK). In some cases you may need to scroll up to **Done** and then press (OK) or tap OK OK to make changes effective.

BLACK AND WHITE PORTRAIT »
Menus give access to an enormous range of options—including monochrome shooting.
110mm, 1/200 sec., f/11, ISO 250.

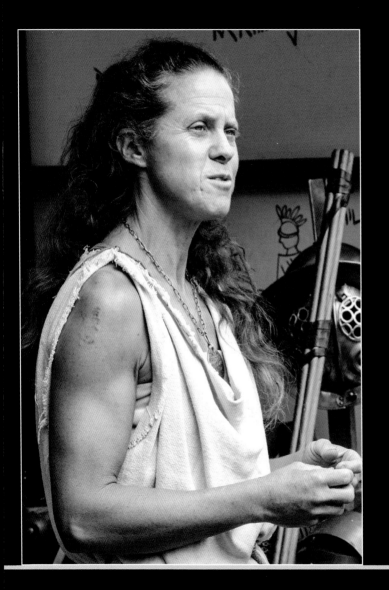

3

Navigating the menus—touch screen

You may well find it quicker to navigate the menus using the touch screen, but you need to be quite precise—I've found it easy to hit the option next to the one I actually want.

1) To display the main menu screen, press **MENU**.

2) Tap the icon for the required menu in the strip on the left of the screen.

3) Tap a specific menu item to see its options. If the menu item you want is not visible, swipe with a finger to scroll up or down.

4) Tap the desired setting to select it. In some cases you may need to tap OK OK to make changes effective.

5) You can exit at any point by pressing **MENU** or tapping ⤺ .

> **Tip**
>
> *You can access help from within most menu items by pressing ⊖ ▓ or tapping ❓.*

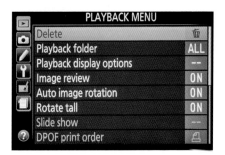

The D5500's Playback menu contains 10 items that affect how images are viewed, stored, shared, deleted, and printed. Most of these are only accessible when a memory card—with image(s)—is present in the camera.

› Delete

This function allows images stored on the memory card to be deleted, either singly or in batches.

1) In the Playback menu, choose **Delete**.

2) In the menu options screen, choose **Selected**, **Select date**, or **All**.

3) If you choose **Selected**, images in the active playback folder or folders (see next page) are displayed as thumbnail images. Use the multi-selector or tap the screen to highlight an image. Press ⊕ or tap ❓Zoom for a larger view of the highlighted image. Press ⊖▦ to mark this image for deletion (you might think you'd use 🗑, but you can't). It will be tagged with a 🗑 icon. If you change your mind, highlight a tagged image and press ⊖▦ again to remove the tag.

4) Repeat this process to select further images. Press (OK) or tap ⨀OK OK to see a confirmation screen. Tap **YES**, or select it and press (OK) to delete the selected image(s). To exit without deleting any images, select **NO**.

5) If you choose **Select date**, you'll see a list of dates on which images on the memory card were taken. Highlight a date and press ▶ or tap the check box to mark it for deletion. If you change your mind, repeat the operation to remove the tag.

6) Repeat this procedure to select further dates. Press (OK) or tap ⨀OK OK to see a confirmation screen. Tap **YES**, or select it and press (OK) to delete all image(s) taken on the selected date(s); to exit without deleting any images, select **NO**.

› Playback folder

By default, the D5500's playback screen will only display images created on the D5500—if you insert a memory card containing images captured on a different model of camera (even another Nikon DSLR) they will not be visible. This can be changed using this menu.

PLAYBACK FOLDER OPTIONS

D5500	Displays images in all folders created by the D5500.
All (default)	Displays images in all folders on the memory card.
Current	Displays images in the current folder only. (The current or active folder is chosen through the Shooting menu, see page 117.)

> ### Tip
>
> *Individual images can also be deleted from the normal playback screen, and this is usually more convenient (see page 100).*

› Playback display options

This lets you choose what (if any) information about each image is displayed on playback. See page 100 for more, including a table showing all the options.

› Image review

If Image review is **On** (the default setting), images are automatically displayed on the monitor after shooting. If **Off**, images are only displayed by pressing ▶. This can economize battery power.

› Auto image rotation

If set to **On** (default), information about the orientation of the camera is recorded with every photo taken, ensuring that they will appear the right way up when viewed with Nikon View NX2, Nikon Capture NX-D, or most third-party imaging applications.

› Rotate tall

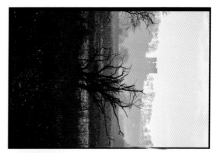

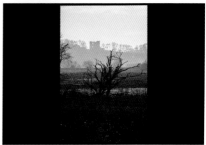

ROTATE TALL OFF/ON ⌃

This determines whether portrait format ("tall") images will be displayed the right way up during playback. If set to **Off**, which is the default, these images will not be rotated, so you'll need to turn the camera through 90° to view them correctly, but they will use the full screen area. If set to **On**, portrait images will be displayed in correct orientation but will appear smaller.

› Slide show

This enables you to display images as a slide show, either on the camera's screen or when it is connected to a TV. All images in the folder or folders selected for playback (see Playback Folder, above) will be played in chronological order.

1) Make sure the playback screen is set to **Image only** (see page 113) to ensure an uncluttered slide show.

2) In the Playback menu, select **Slide show**.

3) Select **Image type** (i.e. still images, movies, or both). You can also select **By rating** to, for example, only include images you've rated with five stars (see below for info on rating images).

4) Select **Frame interval**. You can choose **2**, **3**, **5**, or **10** seconds.

5) Select **Start** and press ⊙K. Or just tap **Start**.

6) When the show ends, a dialog screen is displayed. Tap **Restart**, or select it and press ⊙K to play again. You can also select **Frame interval** (to return to step 4) or **Exit**.

7) If you press ⊙K or tap the screen during the slide show, the slide show is paused and the same screen displayed. The only difference is that if you select **Restart** here, the show will resume where it left off.

› DPOF print order

This allows you to select image(s) to be printed when the camera is connected to, or the memory card is inserted into, a suitable printer, i.e. one that complies with the DPOF (Digital Print Order Format) standard. If there are no JPEG images on the memory card, this menu item is unavailable. For more on printing see Chapter 9 (page 232).

› Rating

This allows you to rate images with one to five stars. Slide show demonstrates one possible use for this. To assign ratings:

1) In the Playback menu, tap **Rating**, or highlight it and press ▶. Images in the current playback folder are displayed as thumbnails.

2) Use ▶/◀ to scroll through the displayed images. Press ⊕ or tap ◙Zoom to view the highlighted image full-screen. Tap the thumbnail image or use ▲ to assign it up to five stars. Use ▼ to reduce a rating.

3) Repeat with further images. When finished, press ⊙K or tap OK OK to exit.

3

› Select to send to smart device

This allows you to select existing images to be uploaded to your smartphone or tablet when you connect through Nikon's Wireless Mobile Utility (see page 226).

1) In the Playback menu, highlight **Select to send to smart device** and press ▶. Images in the current playback folder are displayed as thumbnails.

2) Use the multi-selector to scroll through the displayed images. Press 🔍 or tap 🔍Zoom to see a larger version of the highlighted image. Tap an image, or press 🔍 to select the highlighted shot for upload. The image will be tagged with a ▶ icon. If you change your mind, tap a tagged image or highlight it and press 🔍 again to remove the tag.

3) Repeat this process to select further images. When satisfied, press 🆗 or tap OK OK to exit.

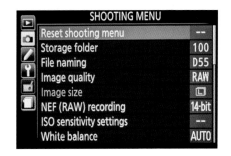

The Shooting menu contains numerous options, but many of these are also accessible through the active information display and have already been discussed.

› Reset shooting menu

This is simply a quick way to restore Shooting menu settings to the camera's original default settings. Use with caution as it can wipe out settings that you have carefully created.

1) In the Shooting menu, tap **Reset shooting menu**, or select it and press 🆗.

2) Tap **Yes**, or select it and press 🆗. Or select **No** to make no changes.

› Storage folder

By default, the D5500 stores images on the memory card in a single folder (named "100D5500"). The camera will automatically create a new folder when the current one becomes full. "Full" means it contains 999 images. If you download your images to your computer regularly and then format the card for reuse, this may never happen.

However, this is possible if you are very prolific or you're traveling for long periods without access to a computer. In this case you might prefer to create an ordered series of folders, perhaps organized by location or date. You might also choose to create specific folders for different shoots or different types of image.

If you alternate different memory cards they can all end up holding folders of the same name. This isn't usually a problem; generally, organizing images on the computer is what matters (see page 229).

Anyway, creating new folder(s) is straightforward.

To create a new folder
1) In the Shooting menu, tap **Storage folder** or select it and press ▶.

2) Tap **New** or select it and press ▶.

3) Name the folder. Only the first three digits are editable and only numbers can be used. If the indicated number is already in use, a "blocked folder" icon appears.

4) When you've set the name, press ⓞⓚ or tap ⓞⓚⓞⓚ to create the new folder. It automatically becomes the active folder. You can also **Rename** an existing folder using a similar process.

To change the active folder
1) In the Shooting menu, tap **Select folder** or select it and press ▶.

2) Scroll through the list (assuming more than one folder exists) and press ⓞⓚ, or simply tap a folder to select it.

› File naming

By default, image files are named as follows: if Color space is sRGB, the name begins "DSC_"; if Color space is AdobeRGB, the name begins "_DSC". This is followed by a four-digit number and a three-letter extension (e.g. ".JPG" for JPEG files). You can edit the initial three-letter string, e.g. replacing it with your initials, so that instead of "DSC_4567.JPG" a file could be "CJS_4567.JPG".

Enter text using the onscreen "keypad". In the past, text entry has been done with the multi-selector, but it is much quicker and more intuitive using the touch screen.

› Image quality

Use this to choose between NEF (RAW) and JPEG options, as described on page 82.

› Image size

Use this to select Image size, as described on page 85. If RAW is selected for Image quality this item is grayed out and cannot be accessed.

› NEF (RAW) recording

This menu offers allows you to set **NEF (RAW) bit depth** to either **12-bit** or **14-bit**. See page 84.

› ISO sensitivity settings

This menu governs ISO sensitivity settings, already discussed in depth on page 69.

› White balance

Allows you to set the white balance, discussed in depth on page 77.

› Set Picture Control and Manage Picture Control

These menus govern the use of Nikon Picture Controls, discussed in depth on page 105.

› Color space

This menu allows you to choose between sRGB and Adobe RGB color spaces (see page 81).

› Active D-lighting

This governs the use of Active D-Lighting, discussed in depth on page 104.

› HDR (high dynamic range)

This enables and controls HDR shooting, as described on page 108.

› Release mode

This menu governs release mode options, and offers the same choices as using 🖳 (see page 34).

› Long exposure NR

Photos taken at long shutter speeds can suffer from increased "noise" (page 69) and the D5500 therefore offers the option of extra image processing to counteract this.

If Long exposure noise reduction (its full name) is **On**, it applies at exposure times of 1 sec. or longer. During image processing, *Job nr* flashes in the viewfinder. The time taken is equal to the shutter speed in use, and no further pictures can be taken until processing is complete.

This causes significant delays in shooting and many users prefer to tackle image noise in post-processing. Long exposure noise reduction is **Off** by default.

› High ISO NR

Photos taken at high ISO settings can also show significant noise. The default setting is **Normal**, which can be changed to **Low** or **High**. High ISO NR can also be set to **OFF**, but even then a modest amount of NR will be applied to images taken at the highest ISO settings.

Tip

High levels of NR will remove noise very effectively, but can also smooth the image so much that it looks "plastic" and loses any semblance of fine detail. With JPEG images, you can't restore any of the lost texture or detail. It's better to apply noise-reduction in post-processing, when you can see the effect more clearly and undo if necessary.

› Vignette control

Vignetting is a darkening towards the corners of the image, most obvious in even-toned areas like clear skies. Almost all lenses show slight vignetting at maximum aperture. It usually reduces or disappears when the lens is stopped down. The D5500 can compensate for vignetting during the in-camera processing of JPEG images (not RAW files or movies). Vignette control only operates with DX lenses of Type D, G, or E (see page 203). Use this menu to choose between **Normal** (the default setting), **High**, **Low**, and **Off**.

› Auto distortion control

If **On**, this automatically corrects for distortion (see page 194) which may arise with certain lenses. It's available only with Type D, G, or E lenses (see page 204), excluding fisheye and PC lenses. It only applies to JPEG images, not RAW images or movies.

› Interval timer shooting

The D5500 can take a number of shots at pre-determined intervals. There are various applications for this, most obviously to create a time-lapse movie, although you'll need specialized software to compile the images for this. I've also used the interval timer on occasions as a more flexible self-timer (page 34), for instance, when a 20-second delay isn't long enough.

There are several options within the Interval timer shooting menu. After choosing your settings in each of these screens, press (OK) or tap OK OK to return to the main Interval timer shooting menu.

Start options

If you select **Now**, shooting begins 3 seconds after you complete the other settings. To set a later starting time, select **Choose start day and start time**. You can select any date in the current year.

Interval

The default interval between shots is 1 minute, but you can select any value from 1 second to 24 hours.

Number of times

Select the total number of shots to be taken (up to 9999). The total number of shots that this amounts to is also displayed. Press ▶ to complete the setup and reach the primary Interval timer shooting screen.

Exposure smoothing

Exposure smoothing aims to minimize brightness differences between successive shots, e.g. if light levels change. These can cause very distracting flicker effects in a time-lapse movie. Exposure smoothing is not applicable in mode M unless Auto ISO sensitivity control is enabled (page 70). When you've completed these settings, return to the main Interval timer shooting menu and tap **Start**, or highlight it and press ▶.

If you want to cancel an interval timer sequence before the end, there are several options. The simplest is just to turn the camera off and on again. If you return to the Interval timer shooting menu after this you will see options for **Restart** or **Off**.

Note:

If you're planning a large number of shots, and/or long intervals, ensure that the battery is fully charged or the camera is connected to a mains adapter, and that there is sufficient space on the memory card. If the card becomes full during an Interval timer sequence, shooting stops until the card is replaced.

› Movie settings

Sets key options for movie shooting (see page 174).

» CUSTOM SETTING MENU

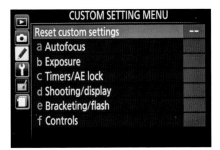

The Custom Setting menu allows you to fine-tune almost every aspect of the camera's operation to suit your personal preferences. The menu is divided into six groups or submenus, identified by key letters and a color: **a: Autofocus** (red); **b: Metering/Exposure** (yellow); **c: Timers/AE Lock** (green); **d: Shooting/display** (light blue); **e: Bracketing/flash** (dark blue); and **f: Controls** (lilac).

Navigating the Custom Setting menu is essentially the same as the other menus. However, from the main menu screen, when you first tap on the pencil icon or press ▶ you enter the list of submenus. Tap one of these to see its constituent items, or scroll to the desired group and press ▶.

Although the menu is organized into seven groups, individual items do appear as a continuous list, so you can scroll straight down from **a4** to **b1**, and so on. By scrolling up you can jump directly from from **a1** to **f4**.

The custom setting identifier code (e.g. **a4**) is shown in the appropriate color for that group. If you change the setting from the default value, an asterisk appears over the initial letter of the code.

> ### Tip
>
> *If there are certain Custom settings that you visit frequently, these may be more rapidly accessible via Recent Settings; alternatively, you can opt for My Menu and add them to the list there (see page 142).*

› Reset custom settings

This allows you to restore all Custom Settings to original default values. This of course wipes out all the changes you've made to personalize your camera. I can't imagine I'd ever use it, except perhaps before selling the camera or lending it to someone for an extended period.

› Group a: Autofocus

a1 AF-C priority selection
Normally, in AF-C release mode, the camera can take a picture even if it has not acquired perfect focus (**release priority**). Custom setting a1 allows you to choose **focus priority** instead, so that pictures can only be taken once focus is acquired.

a2 Number of focus points
This governs the number of focus points from which you can choose when selecting the focus point manually (see page 90). By default it uses the full 39 points (**AF39**) but you can also opt to use 11 points (**AF11**). Using the smaller number can speed up the selection process.

> **Note:**
> Even when you select **AF11**, the camera still uses all 39 points for automatic selection, focus tracking, and so on.

a3 Built-in AF-assist illuminator
This determines whether the AF-assist illuminator (see page 91) operates when lighting is poor. The default option is **On**.

a4 Rangefinder
This allows you to use the exposure display for assistance in manual focusing (see page 87). The default setting is **Off**.

› Group b: Metering/Exposure

b1 EV steps for exposure cntrl
This governs the increments which the camera uses for setting shutter speed and aperture, as well as for bracketing and so on. The options are **⅓ step** (default) or **½ step**.

b2 ISO display
By default (i.e. **Off** selected in this menu), the figure displayed towards lower right in the viewfinder shows the number of exposures remaining. Select **On** and it will show the current ISO setting instead. I find this a much more useful piece of information and so always set this to **On**.

› Group c: Timers/AE Lock

c1 Shutter-release button AE-L
This determines whether you can lock exposure by half-pressure on the shutter-release button. By default, this item is **Off**, which means that half-pressure locks focus only (see Focus lock, page 91), and you can only lock exposure with the *AE-L/AF-L* button. Change it to **On**, and half-pressure locks both focus and exposure.

c2 Auto off timers
Governs the interval before the relevant displays turn off when the camera is idle (i.e. when you don't take any pictures, or operate any of the other controls). The

options you can select are **Short**, **Medium**, or **Long**; these set different intervals for different camera functions (see the table below). **Short** is a good choice if you want to economize battery life. You can also set your own Custom intervals for each of these timers.

CUSTOM SETTING C2 AUTO OFF TIMERS

Interval for:	Short	Normal	Long
Playback/menus	20 sec.	1 min.	5 min.
Image review	4 sec.	4 sec.	20 sec.
Live view	5 min.	10 min.	20 min.
Standby timer	4 sec.	8 sec.	1 min.

c3 Self-timer

This item has two submenus governing the operation of the self-timer.

Self-timer delay determines the interval between pressing the button and the shot being taken. The default is **10 sec.**; other options are **2**, **5**, and **20 sec.**

As well as taking a single shot, you can create sequences from one press of the release button. **Number of shots** can be set anywhere from **1** to **9**; if you set any value larger than 1, the interval between successive shots is approximately 4 sec.

c4 Remote on duration (ML-L3)

If you're using the optional ML-L3 remote control (see page 214), this governs how long the camera will remain on standby for a signal from the remote before remote control mode turns **Off**. Options range from **1 min** (default) to **15 min.** This does not apply in Live View/movie shooting.

› Group d: Shooting/display

d1 Exposure delay mode

You can use this setting (**Off** by default) to create a delay of approximately 1 sec. when you press the shutter-release button. This is one way to reduce vibration when shooting on a tripod; alternatives include using the self-timer, remote control, or a mobile device via Wi-Fi (see page 226).

d2 File number sequence

This controls how image numbers are set. If it's **Off**, file numbering is reset to 0001 whenever you insert a new memory card, format an existing card, or create a new storage folder (page 117). If it's **On**, numbering continues from the previous highest number used. **Reset** creates a new folder, and begins numbering from 0001.

d3 Viewfinder grid display

This allows the camera to display grid lines in the viewfinder; these can help you keep the camera level and assist with precise framing. The options are **Off** (default) and **On**. It's a personal choice, but I always enable the grid on any camera I'm using.

d4 Date stamp

This allows you to imprint **Date**, or **Date and time**, on photos (JPEG only) as they are taken. **Date counter** imprints number of days to/from a selected date.

d5 Reverse indicators

This governs how the exposure displays in the viewfinder and information display are shown. By default (**-0+** selected), overexposure is indicated by bars on the right side. **+0-** reverses this so overexposure is on the left. There's no reason to change this setting other than personal preference.

> **Note:**
> Date and time information is always embedded in an image's metadata, without you needing to deface the image.

› Group e: Bracketing/flash

e1 Flash cntrl for built-in flash

This governs how the built-in flash is regulated. The default is **TTL**, which means flash output is regulated automatically by the camera's metering system. If you select **Manual**, you can use a sub-menu to determine the strength of the flash, ranging from **Full** down to **1/32** power.

e2 Auto bracketing set

Bracketing is discussed in detail on page 76. The options are: **AE bracketing** (default), **WB bracketing**, and **ADL bracketing**.

› Group f: Controls

f1 Assign Fn. button

A wide range of functions can be assigned to the **Fn** button. In most cases it's used in conjunction with the command dial: pressing **Fn** activates the active information display and highlights the selected setting. Hold in the button and turn the command dial to change values for that setting. In practice this becomes the quickest way to change values for your chosen setting, whether it's ISO, white balance, or anything else on the list. It's therefore worth thinking about which of these settings you change most frequently; for me it's ISO, by a long way, so I'm happy with the default setting.

CUSTOM SETTING F1 ASSIGN FN BUTTON

QUAL	Hold button and rotate command dial to select image quality/size.	All modes.
ISO sensitivity (default)	Hold button and rotate command dial to select ISO sensitivity.	All modes.
White Balance	Hold button and rotate command dial to select white balance setting.	P, S, A, and M modes only.
Active D-Lighting	Hold button and rotate command dial to select Active D-Lighting setting.	P, S, A, and M modes only.
HDR	Hold button and rotate command dial to choose HDR settings and make next shot an HDR image.	P, S, A, and M modes only; image quality must be set to JPEG.
+NEF (RAW)	When Image quality is set to JPEG, records a NEF copy of the next shot taken.	All modes which support RAW (see page 82).
Auto bracketing	Hold button and rotate command dial to choose bracketing increment or toggle Active D-Lighting On/Off.	P, S, A, and M modes only.
AF-area mode	Hold button and rotate command dial to select AF-area mode.	All modes.
Viewfinder grid display	Hold button and rotate command dial to toggle grid display on/off.	All modes.
Wi-Fi	Press button to open Wi-Fi item in Setup menu.	All modes.

CUSTOM SETTING F2 ASSIGN *AE-L/AF-L* BUTTON

Options		
AE/AF lock (default)	Pressing **AE-L/AF-L** locks both focus and exposure until next shot is taken.	
AE lock only	Pressing **AE-L/AF-L** locks exposure until next shot is taken.	
AE lock (Hold)	Pressing **AE-L/AF-L** locks exposure for all subsequent shots, until you press the button again or the standby timer interval (see page 119) runs out.	
AF lock only	Pressing **AE-L/AF-L** locks focus until next shot is taken.	
AF-ON	Pressing **AE-L/AF-L** activates focus; focus can't be activated with half-press on shutter release.	

f2 Assign *AE-L/AF-L* button

Similarly, you can assign a number of different functions to the **AE-L/AF-L** button.

f3 Assign touch Fn

This allows you to use the touch screen to change certain settings while looking through the viewfinder. To do this you must have **Touch controls** and **Info display auto off** enabled in the Setup menu (as they both are by default). **Info display auto off** means that the eye sensor turns off the information display when you put the camera to your eye. You can then swipe left or right across the screen to adjust the chosen value, which you'll see in

the viewfinder. If you're holding the camera normally, you'll naturally use the right thumb for this.

As with the **Fn** and **AE-L/AF-L** buttons discussed above, it's worth thinking about which options you need to access frequently when the camera is at your eye. For example, as I use Manual mode a lot, I experimented with selecting Aperture for this. However, it takes multiple swipes to change by multiple steps, so it's faster to hold ⊠ while rotating the command dial.

Of all these settings, the one that seems quickest and most intuitive via the touch screen is Focus-point selection.

CUSTOM SETTING F3 ASSIGN TOUCH FN

Focus-point selection	Swipe to select focus point.	AF-S or AF-C must be selected (see page 86).
ISO sensitivity (default)	Swipe to adjust ISO sensitivity.	All modes.
Active D-Lighting	Swipe to select Active D-Lighting setting.	P, S, A, and M modes only.
HDR	Swipe to choose HDR settings and make next shot an HDR image.	P, S, A, and M modes only; image quality must be set to JPEG.
Auto bracketing	Swipe to choose bracketing increment or toggle Active D-Lighting On/Off.	P, S, A, and M modes only.
AF-area mode	Swipe to select AF-area mode.	All modes.
Viewfinder grid display (default)	Swipe to toggle grid display on and off.	All modes.
Aperture	Swipe to adjust aperture.	A and M modes only.

f4 Reverse dial rotation

This reverses the effect of rotating the command dial in a given direction. For instance, in A mode, turning it to the right normally makes the aperture smaller, but you can make it have the opposite effect. You can customize this separately for **Exposure compensation** and for **Shutter speed/aperture** settings.

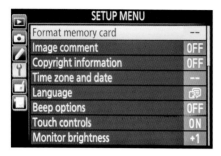

The Setup menu controls various important camera functions, although many are ones you will need to access only occasionally, if at all.

> ## Format memory card

This is the one item in this menu that you are likely to use regularly. The process is outlined on page 23.

> ## Image comment

You can append brief comments (36 characters, or about a quarter of a Tweet) to images. Comments appear in the third info page on playback (see page 100) and can be viewed in Nikon View NX2 and Nikon Capture NX2. To attach a comment, tap **Input comment** or select it and press ▶, then enter text using the onscreen "keypad". As already observed, this is much quicker using the touch screen.

When you've finished entering text, tap

or press ⊕. Tap **Attach comment**, or select **Done** and press ⊛. The comment will be attached to all new shots until turned off again.

> ## Copyright information

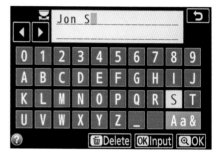

Copyright is a fundamental right, and exists automatically in every photo you take. However, making a clear statement that your images are covered by copyright is still worthwhile. It doesn't confer any additional rights, but can make it easier to enforce your existing rights.

> **Note:**
> Copyright normally exists in any photo you take, without registration. However, in the US and a few other countries, registration—although a cumbersome, bureaucratic process—can help you to enforce your rights.

This menu allows copyright information to be embedded into metadata, using the usual text input method.

There are separate fields for **Artist** (i.e. photographer) and **Copyright**; however, in most jurisdictions, they are usually one and the same person, as copyright automatically belongs to the person creating the image. There is often an exception for photographers shooting in the course of permanent employment (not freelancers under contract), when copyright belongs to the employer. Copyright law does vary internationally, and it is wise to familiarize yourself with the local laws where you work.

To attach copyright information to all subsequent photos, tap **Attach copyright information**, or select it then press (OK).

› Time zone and date

Sets date, time, and time zone, and specifies the date display format (Y/M/D, M/D/Y, or D/M/Y). First set your usual time zone, then set the time correctly. If you travel to a different time zone, change the time zone setting and the time will be corrected automatically.

Note:
If a GPS receiver is attached (see page 230), it can set the clock using the very accurate data from the satellite system. Enable this in the **Location data** submenu (see page 132).

› Language

Sets the language which the camera uses in its menus.

› Beep options

If you wish, the camera can emit a beep when the self-timer operates, and to signify that focus has been acquired when shooting in single-servo AF mode. You can choose a **High** or **Low** pitch for the beep. It's **Off** by default, and quite right too.

› Touch controls

This menu has three options. **Enable** lets you use the touch screen for the full range of operations, including using the active information display, navigating the menus, and playback. The other options are self-explanatory: **Playback only** and **Disable**.

3

› Monitor brightness

This allows you to change the brightness of the LCD display, using ▲/▼ or ▲/▼. Use with care—making review/playback images appear brighter does not mean the images themselves (e.g. as viewed on your computer) will be any brighter.

The point is that you can adapt screen brightness to changing light levels in your surroundings. The screen shows a "step-wedge" with 10 bands ranging from very dark to very light gray. It should be possible to distinguish clearly between all of them.

> **Note:**
> Monitor brightness in Live View/ movie shooting is adjusted separately (see page 175).

› Info display format

This lets you choose between **Graphic** (default) and **Classic** modes for the information display (see page 28). You can also select different background colors.

There are separate options for User-control modes (**P**, **S**, **A**, and **M** modes) and for Auto/Scene/Effects modes; setting a different screen mode, or just a different background color, could be a handy

reminder of which group of modes you're in.

› Auto info display

By default (i.e. this item is **On**), the information display appears automatically when you half-press the shutter-release button. If Image Review is **Off** (page 114), it will also appear immediately after you take a shot.

If you turn this item **Off**, the information display only appears when you press **info**. You can turn it off to conserve battery power, or if you're working entirely through the viewfinder.

› Clean image sensor and Lock mirror up for cleaning

For more details see page 218.

› Image Dust Off ref photo

Nikon Capture NX-D (see page 228) can automatically remove dust spots on images, by comparing them to a reference photo which maps dust on the sensor. This can save a lot of grunt-work compared to manually removing spots from individual images. This menu item allows you to take a suitable reference photo.

To take a dust-off reference photo
1) Fit a lens (preferably at least 50mm

focal length). With a zoom lens, use the longest setting. Locate a featureless white object such as a sheet of paper, large enough to fill the frame.

2) Tap **Image Dust Off Ref Photo** or select it and press ▶.

3) Tap **Start** or **Clean sensor** and then **Start**, or select one and press ▶. (Select **Start** if you have already taken the picture from which you want to remove spots.)

4) Frame the white object at a distance of about 4in. (10cm). Press the shutter-release button halfway; focus is automatically set to infinity, creating a soft white background against which dust spots stand out clearly.

5) Press the shutter-release button fully to capture the reference image.

› Flicker reduction

Some light sources can produce visible flicker in the Live View screen image and in movie recording. To minimize this, use this menu to match the frequency of the local mains power supply. **60Hz** is common in North America, and **50Hz** is normal in the European Union, including the UK. Normally, you can leave this on **Auto** and the camera will adjust automatically.

› Slot empty release lock

By default (**Enable release** selected in this menu), the shutter can be released even if no memory card is present. Images are held in the buffer and can be displayed on the monitor (demo mode), but are not recorded. This is useful when cameras are on display at a shop or trade show, but not in normal use.

Alternatively you can select **Release locked** instead. This means that the shutter can't be released unless there's a memory card in the camera. The obvious lack of response protects you against shooting away happily for hours, only to discover later that none of your images have been recorded.

› Video mode

The name is potentially confusing, as this is not directly related to the camera's Movie mode. You can connect the camera to a TV or VCR to view images; this menu sets the camera to **NTSC** or **PAL** standards to match the device you're connecting to. NTSC is used in North America and Japan, but most of the rest of the world uses PAL.

› HDMI

You can also connect the camera to HDMI (High Definition Multimedia Interface) TVs—you'll need a special cable. This menu sets the camera's output to match the HDMI device (get this information from that device's specs or instructions). The **Device control** submenu applies when connected to an HDMI-CEC television, and allows the TV remote to be used to navigate through images.

› Accessory terminal

This item has two submenus.

Location data
This item regulates the operation of an accessory GPS device (see page 230).

Remote control
This contains options which apply when you're using some of Nikon's remote cords and wireless remote controls, although not the ML-L3 (see page 214).

The first option is **Remote shutter release**. This determines what happens when you press the release button on the remote. You can set it to **Take photos** or **Record movies**.

The second option is **Assign Fn Button**. If the remote has an Fn button, you can set it to **Same as camera *AE-L/AF-L* button** (i.e. it serves the function you've selected in Custom setting f2). Alternatively you can select **Live view**, which means that the remote's Fn button starts and stops Live View.

› Wi-Fi

Use this to enable and regulate the onboard Wi-Fi (see Chapter 9 Connection, page 226).

› Eye-Fi upload

You can also set up a Wi-Fi network connection using an Eye-Fi card (see Chapter 9 Connection, page 229). This menu item is only visible when there's an Eye-Fi card in the memory card slot.

› Conformity marking

Displays some technical standards with which the camera complies. It's for information only; there are no options to choose.

› Firmware version

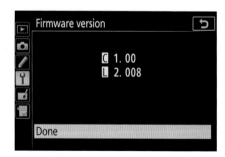

Firmware is the onboard software which controls the camera's operation. Nikon issues updates periodically. This menu shows the version presently installed, so you can verify whether it is current or not. When new firmware is released, download it from the Nikon website and copy it to a memory card. Insert this card in the camera, then use this menu to update the camera's firmware.

Note:
Firmware updates may include new or modified functions and menu items that can make this *Guide* (as well as the Nikon manual) appear out of date.

WILD GEESE ⌄
Either remote control or Wi-Fi may prove useful when photographing shy subjects.
115mm, 1/1000 sec., f/5.6, ISO 800, tripod.

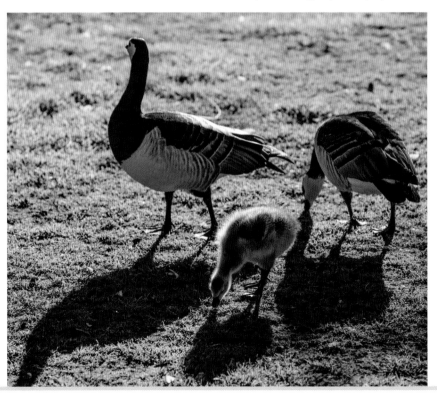

3 **» RETOUCH MENU**

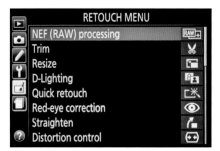

RETOUCH MENU

NEF (RAW) processing
Trim
Resize
D-Lighting
Quick retouch
Red-eye correction
Straighten
Distortion control

The Retouch menu lets you make corrections and enhancements to images, including cropping, color balance, and much more. The original image remains untouched; instead, a copy is created to which the changes are applied. Further retouching can be applied to the new copy, but you can't apply the same effect twice to the same image.

Copies are always created in JPEG format but the size and quality depend on the format of the original (a few exceptions, such as **Trim** and **Resize**, produce copies smaller than the original).

FORMAT OF ORIGINAL PHOTO	QUALITY AND SIZE OF COPY
NEF (RAW)	Fine, Large
JPEG	Quality and size match original

› To create a retouched image

1) In the Retouch menu, select a retouch option. If subsidiary options appear, make a further selection. A screen of image thumbnails appears. Select the required image, as you would during normal image playback. A preview of the retouched image appears.

2) Alternatively, from image playback, highlight the image you'd like to retouch. Press **⊞** and from the next screen select **Retouch**.

3) Depending on the type of retouching to be done (see below), there may be further options to choose from.

4) Press ⊛ or tap ☐OK☐ to see a preview of the results. Press ⊛ or tap ☐OK☐ to create a retouched copy.

> **Note:**
> Retouched copy images are indicated by an ☑ icon in normal image playback.

› NEF (RAW) Processing

This menu creates JPEG copies from images originally shot as RAW files. It doesn't replace full RAW processing on computer (see page 227), but it does allow you to create quick copies for immediate sharing or printing. Processing options (see the table below) are displayed in a column alongside a preview image.

When satisfied with the previewed image, tap **EXE** or select it and press ⓄⓀ to create the JPEG copy. Pressing **MENU** exits without creating a copy.

OPTION HEADING	DESCRIPTION
Image quality	Choose Fine, Normal, or Basic (see pages 82 and 118).
Image size	Choose Large, Medium, or Small (see pages 85 and 118).
White balance	Choose a white balance setting; options are similar to those described on pages 80 and 118.
Exposure compensation	Adjust exposure (brightness) levels from +2 to −2.
Set Picture Control	Choose any of the range of Nikon Picture Controls (see page 105) to be applied to the image. Fine-tuning options can also be applied.
High ISO NR	Choose level of noise reduction where appropriate (see page 118).
Color space	Choose color space (see pages 81 and 118).
Vignette control	Apply Vignette control (see page 119).
D-Lighting	Choose D-Lighting level (High, Normal, Low, or Off) (see page 137).

› Trim

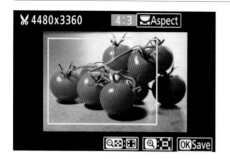

ratio of the crop with the command dial (see the table below). Adjust its size using ⊖□ and ⊕. Shift its position using the multi-selector.

This allows you to crop images to improve framing or to match a specific print size. A preview screen indicates the crop area with a yellow rectangle. Change the aspect

ASPECT RATIO	POSSIBLE SIZES FOR TRIMMED COPY									
3:2 (same as original)	5760 x 3840	5120 x 3416	4480 x 2984	3840 x 2560	3200 x 2128	2560 x 1704	1920 x 1280	1280 x 856	960 x 640	640 x 424
4:3	5328 x 4000	5120 x 3840	4480 x 3360	3840 x 2880	3200 x 2400	2560 x 1920	1920 x 1440	1280 x 960	960 x 720	640 x 480
5:4	5008 x 4000	4800 x 3840	4208 x 3360	3600 x 2880	3008 x 2400	2400 x 1920	1808 x 1440	1200 x 960	896 x 720	608 x 480
1:1	4000 x 4000	3840 x 3840	3360 x 3360	2880 x 2880	2400 x 2400	1920 x 1920	1440 x 1440	960 x 960	720 x 720	480 x 480
16:9	6000 x 3376	5760 x 3240	5120 x 2880	4480 x 2520	3840 x 2160	3200 x 1800	2560 x 1440	1920 x 1080	1280 x 720	960 x 536	64 3€

› Resize

This option creates a small copy of the selected picture(s), suitable for immediate use with various external devices. Four possible sizes are available:

OPTION	SIZE (PIXELS)	POSSIBLE USES
2.5M	1920 x 1280	Display on HD TV, larger computer monitor, recent iPads, iPhone 6.
1.1M	1280 x 856	Display on typical computer monitor, older iPad.
0.6M	960 x 640	Display on standard TV, iPhone 4/5.
0.3M	640 x 424	Display on majority of mobile devices.

› D-Lighting

D-Lighting should not be confused with Active D-Lighting (page 104), although there are similarities in the final effect. Active D-Lighting is applied before shooting, and has an effect on the original exposure; D-Lighting is applied later and simply lightens the shadow areas of the image. The D-Lighting screen shows a side-by-side comparison of the original image and the retouched version; a press on ⊕ zooms in on the retouched version. You can preview and modify the strength of the effect, from **Lo** to **Hi**.

If the camera detects faces in the picture, you can select the **Portrait subjects** box. This will confine the effect to the faces. It works for three faces at most.

› Quick retouch

Provides basic "quick fix" retouching, boosting saturation and contrast. D-Lighting is applied automatically to retain shadow detail. Again, you can adjust the strength of the effect, from **Lo** to **Hi**.

› Red-eye correction

This tackles the notorious problem of "red-eye", caused by on-camera flash (see page 154). This option can only be selected for photos taken using flash. The camera analyzes the photo for evidence of red-eye; if none is found the process ends. If red-eye is detected, a preview image appears; use the zoom controls as usual to view it more closely.

› Straighten

It's best to get horizons level at the time of shooting, and the virtual horizon can help. However, errors can still happen. This option offers a fall-back, with correction up to 5° in 0.25° steps. Use ▶/◀ or touch controls to rotate clockwise/anticlockwise. Inevitably, this crops the image.

› Distortion control

Some lenses create noticeable curvature of straight lines (see page 194); this menu allows you to correct this in-camera. This inevitably crops the image slightly. **Auto** allows automatic compensation for the known characteristics of Type G and D Nikkor lenses (**Auto Distortion control**, in the Shooting menu, can apply this automatically to JPEG images).

If you have images taken with other lenses, you'll have to use **Manual** instead.

› Perspective control

Corrects the convergence of vertical lines in photos taken looking up, for example, at tall buildings. Grid lines help you assess the effect, and you control its strength with the multi-selector or touch controls. The process inevitably crops the image, so leave room around the subject when you shoot. For alternative approaches to perspective control, and an illustration, see page 202.

› Fisheye

Instead of correcting distortion, this option exaggerates barrel distortion to give a (not totally convincing) fisheye lens effect. Use the multi-selector or touch controls to vary the effect.

› Filter effects

Mimics several common photographic filters (perhaps we should say once common in the days of film). **Skylight** reduces the blue cast which can affect photos taken on clear days with a lot of blue sky. Applied to other images its effect is very subtle, even undetectable. **Warm filter** has a much stronger warming effect. **Red**, **Green**, and **Blue intensifier** are all fairly self-explanatory, as is **Soft**.

Cross screen, however, is an enigmatic name—surely "Star" would have been better? It creates a "starburst" effect around light sources and other very bright points, like sparkling highlights on water. There are multiple options within this item, including the number, angle, and length of the star points.

› Monochrome

Creates a monochrome copy, as a straight **Black-and-white**, **Sepia** (a brownish toned effect), or **Cyanotype** (a bluish toned effect) image. For **Sepia** or **Cyanotype**, you can make the toning effect stronger or weaker with ▲/▼.

› Image overlay

Image overlay allows you to combine two existing photos into a new image. This can only be applied to originals in RAW format. Nikon claim that the results are better than combining the images in applications like Photoshop because Image overlay makes direct use of the raw data from the camera's sensor, but this is highly debatable. Certainly, a large calibrated computer screen gives you a much better preview of the result.

To create an overlaid image

1) In the Retouch menu, tap **Image overlay** or select it and press ⊙. The next screen has panels labeled **Image 1**, **Image 2**, and **Preview**. Tap **Image 1** or select it and press ⊙.

2) The camera displays thumbnails of RAW images on the memory card. Tap the first image required for the overlay or select it and press ⊙.

3) Tap **Image 2** or press ▶ then ⊙. Select the second image.

4) Use the **Gain** control below each image to determine its "weight" in the final overlay. The preview changes to show the effect.

5) Tap **Overlay** or select it and press ⊙ to preview the result. To save the combined image, tap **Save** or select it and press ⊙.

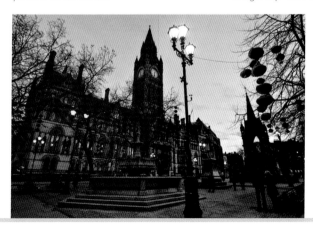

MONOCHROME   «
A comparison of Sepia (left) and Cyanotype (right). Both effects are used here at the strongest setting.

› Color outline

This detects edges in the photograph and uses them to create a "line-drawing" effect. There are no options to alter the effect.

› Photo illustration

This simplifies colors and adds dark outlines where there are clear borders in the image. You can reduce or increase the **Thickness** of these outlines.

› Color sketch

This creates a copy resembling a colored pencil drawing. Controls for **Vividness** and **Outlines** adjust the strength of the effect. Also available as a Special Effect (page 57) when shooting.

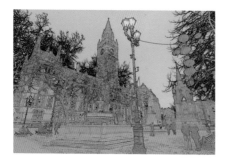

COLOR SKETCH
Vividness and Outlines have both been set to maximum.

› Miniature effect

This option mimics the fad for shooting images with extremely localized depth of field, making real scenes look like miniature models. It usually works best with photos taken from a high viewpoint, which typically have clearer separation of foreground and background. A yellow rectangle shows the area which will remain in sharp focus. You can reposition and resize this using the multi-selector or touch controls. Press and hold 🔍 to preview the results, and tap tap `OK OK` or press 🆗 to save a retouched copy. Also available as a Special Effect (page 58) when shooting.

› Selective color

You can select up to three specific color(s) to be preserved in the retouched copy, while any other hues are transformed to monochrome. Also available as a Special Effect (page 58) when shooting.

1) Use the multi-selector or tap to place the yellow square over an area of the desired color. Press *AE-L/AF-L* to choose that color.

2) To select another color, tap the next "swatch" or turn the command dial to highlight it. Repeat steps 1 and 2.

3) To save the retouched copy, press 🆗 or tap `OK OK` .

› Painting

Another effect in similar vein to Color sketch or Photo illustration, producing an (allegedly) "painterly" result. There are no options to control the effect.

› Edit movie

This grandly titled item merely allows you to trim the start and/or end of movie clips. It's nothing like proper editing (see page 184), but has its uses.

To trim a movie clip:
1) Select a movie clip in full-frame playback. Tap OKPlay or press (OK) to play it.

2) At the point where you want the trimmed clip to start or end, tap anywhere on screen or press (OK) to pause playback.

3) Press ⊞ to reveal an Edit movie options screen.

4) Tap **Choose start/end point** or select it and press (OK). In the next screen tap **Start point** or **End point** or select one and press (OK).

5) The screen now shows the selected start/end frame. If you're happy to start or end the new clip here, tap (OK) or press ▲.

6) You can now opt to **Save as new file** to create a trimmed copy while retaining the original. Alternatively select **Overwrite existing file** to save the trimmed copy and delete the original (careful: there's no going back!)

7) If you get to step 4 then decide to change the start/end frame, tap either of the forward/back arrows on screen, or press ◄/► to play forward or backward. Rotate the command dial to jump forward or back in 10-second steps. When you reach the desired point, tap (OK) or press ▲ and refer to step 5.

8) Repeat if necessary to trim the other end of the clip.

› Side-by-side comparison

This option is not part of the regular Retouch menu—it is only available in playback, when a retouched copy, or its source image, is highlighted. Press ⊞ and from the next screen select **Retouch**. Scroll to **Side-by-side comparison** and tap it or press ► again.

The screen now shows the copy alongside the original source image. Highlight either image with ◄ or ► and press ⊕ to view it full frame.

3 » RECENT SETTINGS AND MY MENU

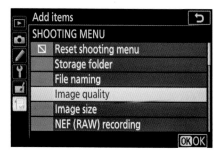

My Menu and Recent Settings share the bottom position in the sidebar of the main menu screen. To choose which is active, follow the **Choose tab** procedure below.

Recent Settings automatically stores the most recent items that you have accessed from any of the other menus, providing a quick way to access controls that you have used recently. The list contains up to 20 items and so is likely to include any that you visit frequently.

My Menu lets you create a customized list of your "favorite" menu items. You do need to add items manually, but it does mean that your preferred items are always there. You can even order them so that your favorites are always at the top. Again, it can store a maximum of 20 items.

› Choose tab

1) In My Menu or Recent Settings (whichever is currently active), tap **Choose tab** or select it and press ▶.

2) Tap the menu you want to activate, or select it and press ⊛.

› To add items to My Menu

1) Tap **Add items**, or select it and press ▶.

2) A list of the other menus now appears. Tap the appropriate menu, or select it and press ▶.

3) Tap the desired menu item, or select it and press ▶.

4) A **Choose position** screen reappears with the newly added item at the top. Use ▲/▼ to reposition it in the list if desired. Press ⊛ or tap OKOK to confirm and save the list.

5) Repeat to add more items.

› To remove items from My Menu

1) Tap **Remove items**, or select it and press ▶.

2) Tap any item, or highlight it and press ▶ to select it for deletion. A check mark appears beside the item.

3) Select additional items in the same way.

4) Press (OK) or tap OK OK . A confirmation dialog appears. To confirm the deletion(s) press (OK) or tap OK OK again. To exit without deleting anything, press **MENU**.

> ### Tip
>
> *A quicker way to delete a single item is to highlight it using the multi-selector, then press 🗑. To confirm deletion press 🗑 again.*

› To rearrange items in My Menu

1) Highlight **Rank items** and press ▶.

2) Highlight any item.

3) Use ▲ or ▼ to move the item up or down; a yellow line shows where its new position will be. Press (OK) or tap OK OK to confirm the new position.

4) Repeat steps 2 and 3 to move further items. When finished, press **MENU** or ↄ to exit.

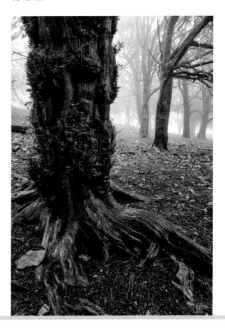

INTO THE WOODS »
Either My Menu or Recent Settings can speed up access to often-used or favorite functions, like the self-timer, which was used here to minimize vibration.
14mm, 4 sec., f/11, ISO 100, tripod.

FLASH

Flash can be immensely useful, and the D5500 has impressive capabilities, as it is integrated with Nikon's acclaimed Creative Lighting System (CLS). However, flash is far from being the answer to every low-light shot. Understanding its limitations helps us understand when to seek alternatives, as well as when and how we can use flash effectively.

» PRINCIPLES

All flashguns are small. All flashguns are weak. These two facts are the keys to understanding flash photography. They are especially true for built-in units like that on the D5500 and most other DSLRs (those on compact cameras are typically even smaller and weaker).

Because it's small, the flash produces very hard light. It's similar to direct sunlight, but even the strongest sunlight is slightly softened by scattering and reflection. We can use the same principles to soften the flash, too.

The weakness of flash is even more fundamental. All flashguns have a limited range, and on-camera flash is more limited than most accessory flashguns.

Built-in flash units raise a third issue, too. Their fixed position, close to the lens, makes the light one-dimensional—and the same for every shot, which is boring. See more on the built-in flash on page 146.

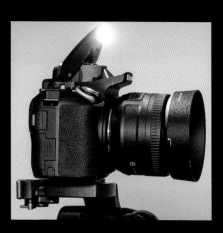

THE BUILT-IN FLASH IN USE　　　　　　　　⌃

TORCHLIGHT　　　　　　　　»
The welding torch was extremely bright but I needed strong flash to balance the image by filling in the areas the torch didn't illuminate.
120mm, 1/80 sec., f/13, ISO 500.

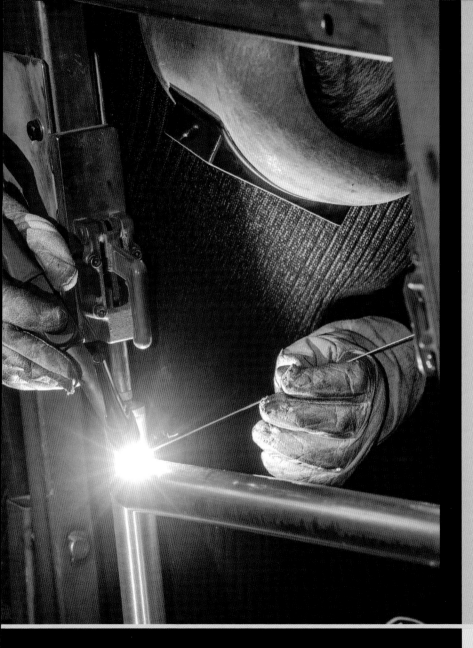

» BUILT-IN FLASH

» FILL-IN FLASH

As just observed, the built-in flash has a limited range, and its flat, harsh light is rarely pleasing. It's certainly better than nothing at times, but its real value is for fill-in light (see below). In ▶ Auto, and many of the Scene modes, the flash activates when the camera deems it necessary (Auto flash), although it can always be turned off. In ⚡ Auto (flash off), and many Scene and Effects modes, the built-in flash is not available. In **P**, **S**, **A**, or **M** modes and 🍴 Food, the flash is always available but you must activate it manually by pressing ⚡.

When you do this, the flash will pop up and begin charging. When it is charged the ready indicator ⚡ is displayed in the viewfinder. Choose a flash mode if required (see page 151) and then take photo(s) in the normal way.

When finished with the built-in flash, press it gently down until it clicks into place.

A key application for flash is for "fill-in" light, giving a lift to dark shadows like those cast by direct sunlight. This is why pros regularly use flash in bright sunlight (often mystifying the uninitiated).

Fill-in flash doesn't need to make the shadows as bright as the sunlit areas, only to lighten them a little. This means the flash can be used at a smaller aperture, or greater distance, than when it's the main light — averaging around 2 Ev smaller, or four times the distance. And, thanks to Nikon's flash metering (i-TTL balanced fill-flash for DSLR), the camera is pretty good at managing this automatically.

Tip

The built-in flash is recommended for use with CPU lenses between 18mm and 300mm focal length. Some lenses may block part of the flash output at close range—removing the lens hood often helps. The Nikon manual details limitations of use with certain lenses.

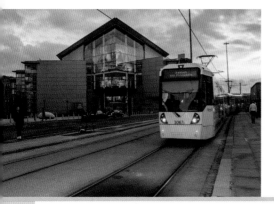

SHADOW «
Even with the lens hood removed, the built-in flash can throw a very obvious shadow, as in the foreground here.
18mm, 1/125 sec., f/8, ISO 800.

› i-TTL balanced fill-flash for DSLR

Nikon's i-TTL balanced fill-flash helps achieve natural-looking results when using fill-in flash. A short series of virtually invisible pre-flashes is used, and light reflected from these is analyzed by the metering sensor to set the flash level.

This will apply automatically, provided (a) matrix or center-weighted metering is selected and (b) a CPU-equipped lens is attached. Since most of us will rarely use the other metering modes, and rarely attach non-CPU lenses (see page 188), this means that fill-flash will be in effect most of the time.

FILL-IN FLASH »

The background exposure is the same for both shots.

18mm, 1/125 sec., f/11, ISO 200.

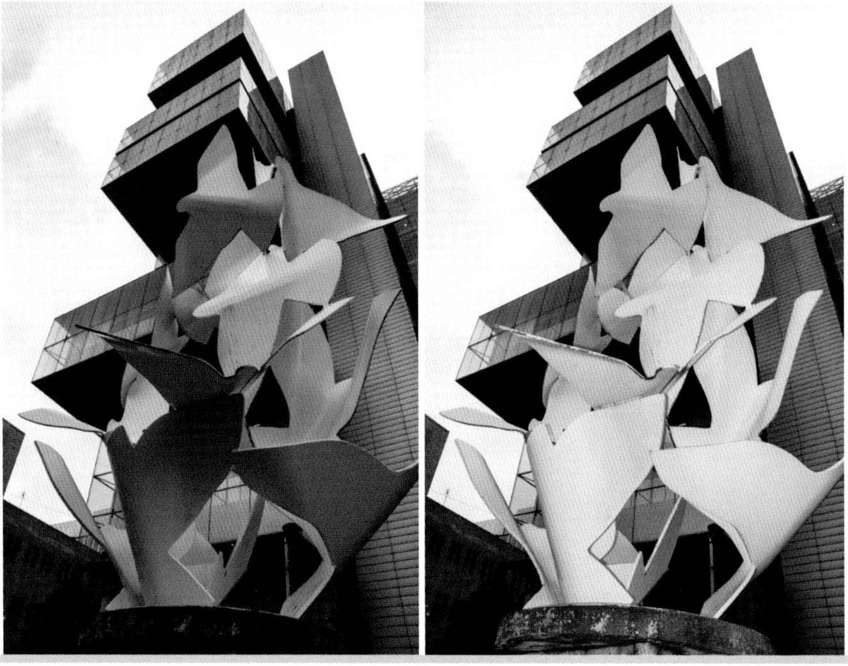

» FLASH EXPOSURE

› Standard i-TTL flash for DSLR

If spot metering is selected, this mode is activated instead (it can also be selected directly on some accessory flashguns). The camera controls flash output to light the subject correctly, but makes no attempt to balance it with background illumination. This is more appropriate when flash is the main light source, rather than providing fill light.

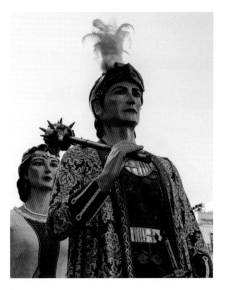

FILL FLASH ⌃
i-TTL balanced fill-flash for DSLR gives a very natural result; it's not overly obvious that flash has been used at all, but without it the detail of the costume would be much less clear.
42mm, 1/160 sec., f/6.3, ISO 100.

Whether the shutter speed is 1/200 sec. or 20 sec., the flash normally fires just once and therefore delivers the same amount of light to the subject. Therefore, if there is no other light, the subject will look the same at any shutter speed. Of course, shooting in total darkness is not normal. Nearly always there will be some other light around. Photographers often call this ambient light.

As soon as there's any ambient light, shutter speed becomes relevant. Slower shutter speeds give ambient light more chance to register.

Aperture, however, affects both flash and ambient exposure. The camera's flash metering takes this into account but it is useful to understand this distinction for a clearer sense of what's going on, especially with slow-sync shots.

The combinations of shutter speed and aperture available when using flash depend on the exposure mode you're using.

EXPOSURE MODE	SHUTTER SPEED	APERTURE
P	Set by camera. The normal range is between 1/200 and 1/60 sec., but in certain flash modes all settings up to 30 sec. are available.	Set by camera.
S	Selected by user. All settings between 1/200 sec. and 30 sec. are available. If you set a faster shutter speed, the D5500 will fire at 1/200 sec. while the flash is active.	Set by camera.
A	Set by camera. The normal range is between 1/200 and 1/60 sec., but in certain flash modes all settings up to 30 sec. are available.	Selected by user.
M	Selected by user. All settings between 1/200 and 30 sec. are available, plus Bulb and Time. If you set a faster shutter speed, the D5500 will fire at 1/200 sec. while the flash is active.	Selected by user.
AUTO, 🌷, 🏔, 🌃, 🐾, 🍴, 🎆, ✨, TOY, VI, POP	Set by camera, between 1/200 and 1/60 sec.	Set by camera.
👤	Set by camera, between 1/200 and 1/30 sec.	Set by camera.
🌆	Set by camera, between 1/200 and 1 sec.	Set by camera.

4 » FLASH RANGE

The usable range of any flash depends on its power, the ISO sensitivity setting, and the aperture selected. If the flash does not reach far enough, you can increase its effective range by setting a higher ISO and/or a wider aperture—but only up to a point.

The table opposite shows the approximate range of the built-in flash for selected distances, apertures, and ISO settings. The table is based on Nikon's own figures, confirmed by practical tests. There's no need to memorize these figures, but it does help to have a general sense of the limited range that always applies when using flash. A quick test shot will tell you if any given subject is within range.

› Guide Numbers

The Guide Number (GN) is a measure of the power of a flash. GNs may be specified in feet or meters. They also vary with the ISO rating. They can be used to calculate flash exposures and working range. With modern flash metering this is rarely necessary, but they do help us compare different flashguns. For instance, the GN for the built-in flash is 12 (meters, ISO 100); for the Nikon SB-910 it is 34, indicating almost three times the power—this allows shooting at three times the distance, at a lower ISO, or with a smaller aperture.

FLASH RANGE «
Although it's around three times more powerful than the built-in flash, a Speedlight SB-700 still has a limited range, creating a bright pool of light in the foreground but having little impact further back.

ISO SETTING						RANGE	
100	200	400	800	1600	3200	meters	feet
1.4	2	2.8	4	5.6	8	1.0-8.5	3ft 3in.-27ft 11in.
2	2.8	4	5.6	8	11	0.7-6.1	2ft 4in.-20ft
2.8	4	5.6	8	11	16	0.6-4.2	2ft-13ft 9in.
4	5.6	8	11	16	22	0.6-3.0	2ft-9ft 10in.
5.6	8	11	16	22	32	0.6-2.1	2ft-6ft 11in.
8	11	16	22	32		0.6-1.5	2ft-4ft 1in.
11	16	22	32			0.6-1.1	2ft-3ft 7in.
16	22	32				0.6-0.7	2ft-2ft 4in.

» FLASH SYNCHRONIZATION AND FLASH MODES

Flash, as the name implies, is virtually instantaneous, lasting just a few milliseconds. If the flash is to cover the whole image frame it must be fired when the shutter is fully open. However, at faster shutter speeds, SLRs including the D5500 do not expose the whole frame at once. In the case of the D5500, the fastest shutter speed which can be used with flash is 1/200 sec. This is therefore known as the sync (for synchronization) speed.

Flash modes are mainly distinguished by how they regulate synchronization and shutter speed. Choose a flash mode from the active information display. Tap the flash icon or highlight it and press ⓞⓚ. Tap the desired flash mode or select it and press ⓞⓚ again.

There is an alternative method: with the flash raised, hold down ⚡ and rotate the command dial until the desired flash mode is shown in the information display.

SETTING FLASH MODE IN THE ACTIVE INFORMATION DISPLAY ⌄

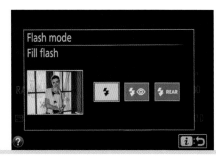

› Standard flash mode (front-curtain sync)

This is the default flash mode in most exposure modes. However, the flash mode item in the active information display labels it **Fill-flash** when using **P**, **S**, **A**, and **M** exposure modes and **Auto flash** in other modes.

In most exposure modes, the camera will automatically set a shutter speed between 1/60–1/200 sec. (see table on page 149). In **S** and **M** exposure modes, you can set any shutter speed down to 30 sec., which means that standard flash also encompasses Slow sync (see below).

This mode may also be called "front-curtain sync" because the flash fires as soon as the shutter is fully open, i.e. as soon as possible after the shutter-release button is pressed.

› Slow sync

This mode allows longer shutter speeds (up to 30 sec.) to be used in **P** and **A** exposure modes, so that backgrounds can be captured even in low ambient light. Movement of the subject or camera (or even both) can result in a partly blurred image combined with a sharp image when the subject is lit by the flash. This may be

SLOW SYNC   ⌄

Slow sync combines a flash image with a motion-blurred image from the ambient light, but front-curtain sync makes the blurred elements run ahead of the flash image (most obvious in the helmet).
24mm, 1/40 sec., f/22, ISO 100.

› Rear-curtain sync

unwanted, but is often used for specific creative effect. You can't select slow sync in **S** and **M** exposure modes, because you can set longer shutter speeds yourself anyway.

A limited version (longest exposure of 1 sec.), labeled Auto slow sync, is available in 🌃 Night portrait mode.

REAR-CURTAIN SYNC ⌄
Rear-curtain sync means that the motion-blurred elements of the image appear behind the sharp image created by the flash.
16mm, 1/60 sec., f/11, ISO 1100.

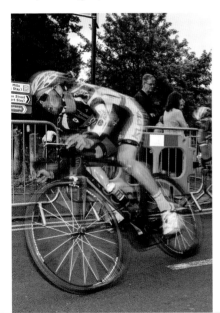

Both standard flash mode and slow sync (above) use front-curtain synchronization, in which the flash fires at the earliest possible moment. This gives a fast response and the best chance of capturing the subject as you see it. However, it can sometimes create odd-looking results when dealing with moving subjects— for these, rear-curtain sync may be more suitable.

Rear-curtain sync triggers the flash not at the first possible instant (as in front-curtain sync) but at the last. With moving subjects, this makes any image created by ambient light appear to trail behind the subject, which usually looks more natural than when it extends ahead. In **P** and **A** modes it also allows you to select slow shutter speeds (below 1/60 sec.), becoming slow rear-curtain sync.

At slow shutter speeds, rear-curtain sync is tricky, as you need to predict where your subject will be at the end of the exposure, rather than at the moment you press the shutter-release button.

4

› Red-eye reduction

On-camera flash, especially from built-in units, often creates "red-eye", when light reflects off the subject's retina. Red-eye reduction works by shining a light (the AF-assist illuminator) at the subject just before the exposure, causing the subject's pupils to contract. This causes a delay, making it unsuitable for moving subjects and killing spontaneity. It's usually better to remove red-eye using Red-eye correction in the Retouch menu (see page 137) or on the computer. Alternatively, use a separate flash, or raise the ISO rating and avoid flash altogether.

Red-eye reduction is on by default in Party/indoor, but fortunately this can be changed.

› Red-eye reduction with slow sync

This combines the two modes named, allowing backgrounds to register. This may help shots look more natural than red-eye reduction mode alone, but is still subject to delay.

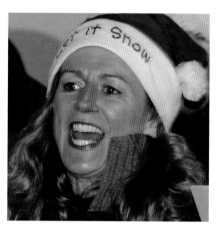

RED-EYE ⌃
Red-eye is unflattering at best, but there are several ways to combat it.
56mm, 1/25 sec., f/5, ISO 1600, Speedlight mounted in hotshoe.

FLASH PAST »
As I was following the fast-moving rider with the camera, there's some blur in the vegetation, but the flash helps to give a generally sharp image of the rider.
85mm, 1/200 sec., f/8, ISO 200, flash.

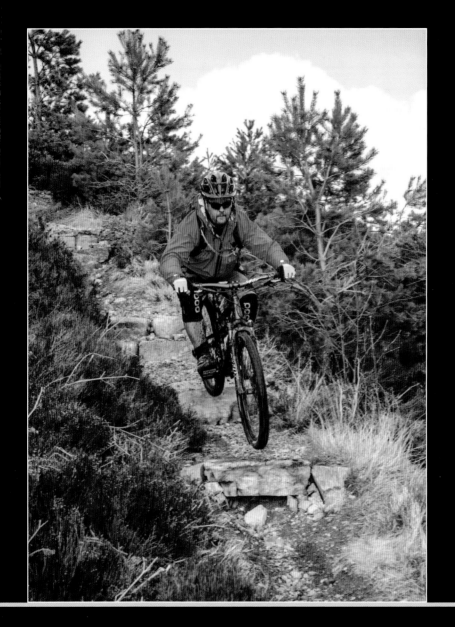

» FLASH COMPENSATION

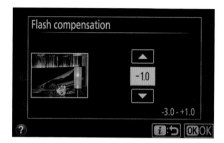

SETTING FLASH COMPENSATION IN THE ⌃ ACTIVE INFORMATION DISPLAY

Although the D5500 has excellent flash metering, it's not infallible. You may also want to adjust flash output for creative effect. Flash compensation works with compatible Speedlights or the built-in flash.

Flash compensation is activated via the active information display; the procedure is just like setting exposure compensation (page 74). Alternatively, press ⚡ and ⧄ and rotate the command dial. This requires some dexterity, but can be quicker.

Compensation can be set from −3 Ev to +1 Ev in increments of ⅓ Ev. Negative compensation reduces the brightness of flash-lit areas, but has no effect on areas lit by other light sources (ambient light).

VIEWPOINT ⌄
The overall exposure was set to capture the rich colors of the sky and the distant landscape, and I carefully checked flash level to ensure that the figure and the boulder did not appear over-lit. *35mm, 0.4 sec., f/11, ISO 100, flash, tripod.*

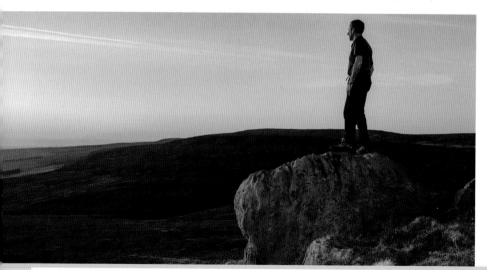

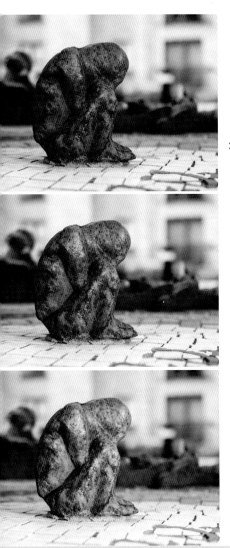

Positive compensation will brighten areas lit by the flash, while leaving other areas unaffected. However, if the subject is already at the limit of flash range, positive compensation can't make it any brighter.

After use, reset flash compensation to zero.

› Manual flash

The Manual option in **Custom setting e1**, Flash cntrl for built-in flash, lets you control flash output precisely, from full power to as low as 1/32. With an external Speedlight, use the unit's own controls.

SCULPTURE   «
The background exposure remains the same, but the flash level on the sculpture varies, with compensation set (from top to bottom) to −1, 0, and +1, respectively.
60mm, 1/200 sec., f/5.6, ISO 250.

» ACCESSORY FLASHGUNS

Compared to the built-in flash, accessory flashguns, which Nikon calls Speedlights, bring much greater power and flexibility. Nikon Speedlights integrate with Nikon's Creative Lighting System for outstanding results. Independent makers such as Sigma offer alternatives, many of them also compatible with i-TTL flash control.

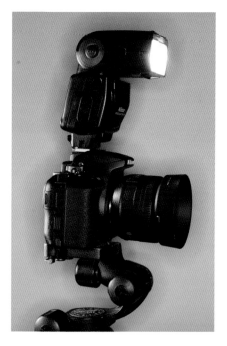

NIKON D5500 AND SPEEDLIGHT SB-700 ⌃

› Using non-Nikon units

Nikon issues dire warnings against using other brands of flash, and it's true that some flashguns may use too high a trigger voltage or even the wrong polarity, which could damage the camera's circuitry. It's best to avoid mounting or connecting any non-Nikon flashgun unless it's from a reputable maker like Sigma or Metz, and their information clearly states that it is compatible.

Some flashguns have a "zoom" feature in the flash head. This means that the coverage, or spread of light, can change to match the angle of view of the lens. Narrowing the beam concentrates the light and so increases the range, which can be helpful when using longer lenses. Units like Nikon's SB-910 and SB-700 zoom automatically to match the lens; the SB-910 does so between 17–200mm. Other units have a fixed angle. The Nikon SB-300 covers the field of an 18mm lens. You can, of course, use much longer lenses with it but the coverage of the flash doesn't change so there's no increase in range.

› Nikon Speedlights and Creative Lighting System

Nikon's Creative Lighting System (CLS), launched in 2003, made flash photography easier and more flexible through innovations including i-TTL flash metering, FV lock, advanced wireless control, and (on some cameras, though not the Nikon D5500) flash synchronization at high shutter speeds.

CLS requires a compatible camera (such as the D5500) and one or more compatible flashguns. These include all current Nikon Speedlights plus several earlier models (SB-900, SB-800, SB-600, and SB-400). The current Speedlights are listed in detail in the table on the next page.

Many older Nikon flashguns can also be used with the D5500 but advanced CLS functions will not be available and the camera will need to be in either S or M exposure mode. The Nikon D5500 manual (which can be downloaded from Nikon websites) gives details.

SPEEDLIGHT SB-300

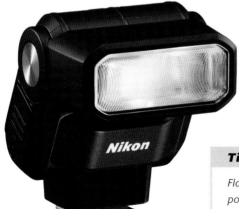

Tip

Flashguns are greedy for battery power. It is always wise to carry at least one set of spares.

› Nikon Speedlights

The table below summarizes the key features of current Nikon Speedlights.

	SB-910	SB-700	SB-500	SB-300	SB-R200
Flash coverage (lens focal length range) with D5500	17–200mm	24–120mm	16mm	18mm	16mm
Guide Number (meters, ISO 100)	34	28	24	18	10
Tilt/swivel	Yes	Yes	Yes	Tilt only	No
Dimensions (width x height x depth, mm)	78.5 x 145 x 113	71 x 126 x 104.5	67 x 114.55 x 70.8	57.4 x 65.4 x 62.3	80 x 75 x 55
Weight (without batteries)	510g	360g	273g	120g	120g
Use as commander?	Yes	Yes	Yes	No	No (cannot be used in camera hotshoe, only as a slave)

› BOUNCE FLASH AND OFF-CAMERA FLASH

Mounting a flashgun in the hotshoe is a start, but its light is still harsh and still quite close to the lens axis, and red-eye remains a common issue.

You can dramatically alter the quality of flash light by bouncing it off a ceiling, wall or reflector or by taking the flashgun off the camera entirely.

› Bounce flash

Bouncing the flash light off a suitable surface spreads the light, softening the shadows, and changes its direction, giving more varied and interesting results.

Many flashguns have heads which can be tilted and swiveled, allowing light to be bounced off walls, ceilings, and other surfaces. Most surfaces will absorb some light, and the light also has to travel further

to reach the subject; i-TTL metering will compensate, but the working range is reduced.

› Off-camera flash

Taking the flashgun off the camera gives complete control over the direction of its light. The flash can be fired wirelessly (see below) or using a flash cord; Nikon's dedicated cords (see page 163) preserve i-TTL metering.

FLASH COMPARISON ⌄
The first shot was taken using the built-in flash; there's an ugly shadow, yet the subject itself looks a bit flat. The second uses off-camera flash high on the left, giving a more 3D result. The third uses bounce flash, giving a softer, more even light.
70mm, f/11, ISO 100, tripod.

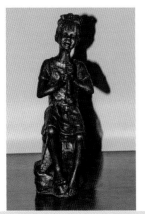 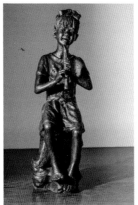 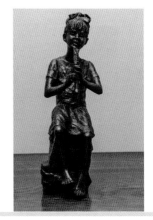

4

› Wireless flash

Nikon's Creative Lighting System includes the ability to regulate the light from multiple Speedlights through a wireless system. The built-in flash units on professional DSLRs like the D800 can be used as the "commander" for a wireless setup, as can SB-910, SB-700, and SB-500 Speedlights. There's also a stand-alone commander, the SU-800, but the SB-500 is the most affordable option.

The D5500 can operate within such a system but must be physically connected to a commander unit such as the SB-500. There are alternative wireless systems too, like Pocket Wizard and Phottix Odin.

WIRELESS FLASH ⌄
The camera was set up on a tripod while I stood a few yards to the right holding an SB-700 flashgun. I used the Phottix Odin radio system to control the flash. Very similar results are possible using a sync lead, although a wireless system gives the photographer more freedom to move around. I reduced the ambient exposure slightly to darken the background.
16mm, 1/15 sec., f/11, ISO 100, tripod.

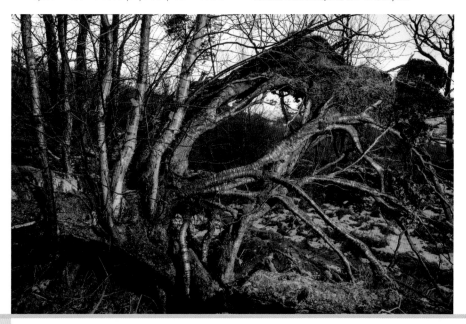

›› FLASH ACCESSORIES

Flash accessories, such as diffusers, reflectors, and remote leads, allow yet more flexibility and control over lighting effects, while power packs increase flash capacity.

› Speedlight Stand AS-19

Allows Speedlights to stand on flat surfaces or mount on a tripod.

› Color filters

Flash filters can be used to create striking color effects, or to match the color of the flash to that of the background lighting. Nikon produces various filters to fit its Speedlight range.

› Flash cords

Because the D5500's built-in flash can't act as a wireless commander, you can only maintain full metering and control of an external Speedlight if it's physically connected to the camera, either in the hotshoe or using a flash cord (also known as a sync lead). Dedicated cords like Nikon's SC-28 allow full communication between camera and Speedlight, retaining i-TTL flash control. The SC-28 extends up to 8ft (2.5m).

› Flash diffusers

Flash diffusers are a simple, economical way to spread and soften the hard light from a flash head. Many flashguns are supplied with a small dome-type diffuser; larger third-party units like those from Honl give almost a "soft-box" effect. For an example, see page 168.

Diffusers inevitably reduce the light reaching the subject; flash metering will compensate, but the effective range is reduced.

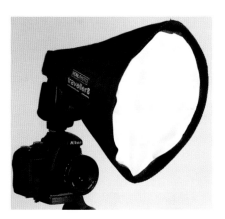

A D5500 AND HONL "SOFTBOX" ⌃

5

CLOSE-UP

Close-up photography is a fascinating branch of the craft, but it certainly has its challenges. A key issue is depth of field (see page 92), which becomes narrower as you move closer to the subject.

This often necessitates using small apertures, which can make long exposures essential. Narrow depth of field also means that the slightest movement of either subject or camera can completely ruin focus. For both reasons, you'll often need a tripod or other solid camera support. Sometimes you'll want to immobilize the subject too (within ethical limits, of course).

With minimal depth of field, focusing becomes critical. Rather than merely focusing on "the subject", you must decide which part of the subject— for instance, an insect's eye or the stamen of a flower— to focus on. The D5500's 39 AF points cover a good spread, but Live View has much to offer. In Live View (see page 96) you can set the focus point anywhere in the frame, and you can zoom in for greater precision. This also makes manual focus both easy and ultra-precise, and I almost never use AF for macro work.

» MACRO PHOTOGRAPHY

"Close-up" is a vague term, but "macro" has a precise meaning: it strictly means photographing objects at a reproduction ratio (see page 166) of 1:1 or better. Many lenses are badged "macro" when their reproduction ratio is only 1:4, or 1:2 at best. There's still plenty of close-up potential, but it isn't classical macro.

You can explore true macro photography without the expense of a dedicated macro lens (see page 169).

BRUSHWORK   »
Most photography is about capturing what you can see with the naked eye. Close-up photography goes beyond this into a whole new world, or at least a new way of seeing the world. *125mm, 1/60 sec., f/6.3, ISO 2000.*

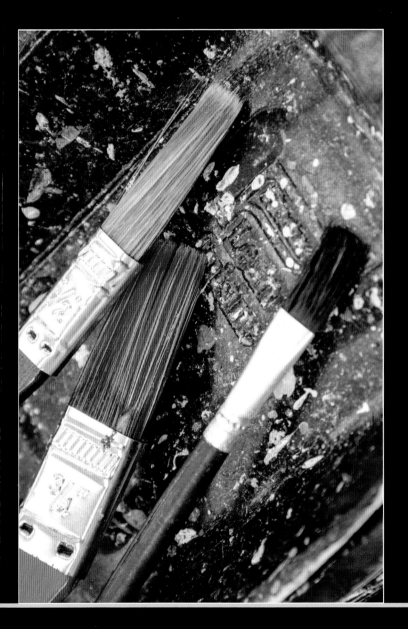

5 » REPRODUCTION RATIO

The reproduction ratio is the ratio between the actual size of the subject and the size of its image on the D5500's imaging sensor, which measures 23.5 x 15.6mm. At 1:1, an object of this size (smaller than an SD memory card) fills the image exactly. When the image is printed, or displayed on a computer screen, it may appear far larger, but that's another story.

A 1:4 reproduction ratio means that the smallest subject to give a frame-filling shot is four times as long/wide as the sensor. With DX-format cameras like the D5500 this is approximately 3.7 x 2.5 inches (94 x 62mm)—slightly larger than a credit card.

FIGURINE ⌄

The first shot has a reproduction ratio of approximately 1:4. The second, taken with a macro lens at minimum distance, gives approximately life size (1:1) reproduction. *70mm and 100mm macro, 1/4 sec., f/5.6, ISO 800.*

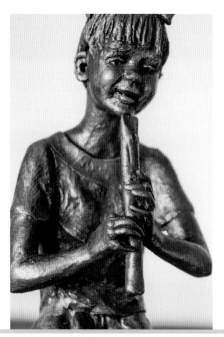
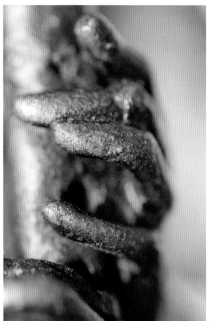

» WORKING DISTANCE

The working distance is the distance required for a desired reproduction ratio with any given lens. It relates directly to the focal length of the lens: a 200mm lens doubles the working distance for 1:1 reproduction compared to a 100mm. Extra distance can help when photographing mobile subjects and ones which might be damaged by accidental contact. It also makes it easier to get good light onto the subject.

Tip

Working distance, like a lens's minimum focus distance, is measured from the focal plane, effectively the surface of the sensor. A 9in. (25cm) working distance can put the subject, or key part of the subject, less than 4in. (10cm) from the front of the lens. Lens hoods or ring-flash can narrow this gap even more.

» MACRO LIGHTING

The built-in flash activates automatically in 🌷 Close up mode, yet it's all but useless for real macro photography, as the lens partly blocks its light with really close subjects. Shadows—your own, or the camera's—often intrude when you're using available light, too. With macro subjects, almost more than any others, it's often crucial to direct the light exactly where it's needed.

Ring-flash units encircle the lens, giving even illumination on ultra-close subjects (they're also favored by some portrait photographers). They are available from Sigma, Nissin, and others.

Nikon prefers a twin-flash approach with its Speedlight Commander Kit R1C1 and

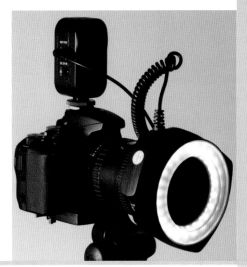

RING LIGHT »
D5500 and Sunpak LED Macro Ring Light—this is an older version, not the DSLR67.

› LED light

Speedlight Remote Kit R1. Both use Speedlight SB-R200 flashguns, mounting either side of the lens. The R1C1 includes a Wireless Speedlight Commander SU-800, which fits into the camera's hotshoe, while the R1 needs a separate commander. Either way, it's an expensive package.

LED lights, such as the Sunpak DSLR67 LED Macro Ring Light, are a much cheaper alternative. It's only suitable for close subjects, but that's all you need in a macro light. You may still need fairly high ISO ratings to achieve sufficiently fast shutter speeds for mobile subjects.

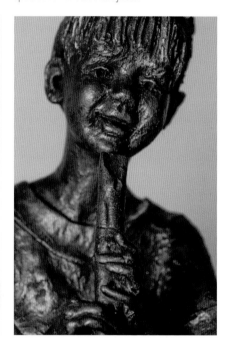

LED RING LIGHTING ⌃
Image taken with the Sunpak LED Macro Ring Light.
100mm macro, 1/30 sec., f/11, ISO 100, tripod.

SOFTBOX LIGHTING ⌃
Comparison image taken with SB-700 flashgun and HONL "softbox", off-camera to the left and fired via remote cord, using the same settings as the previous shot.

» EQUIPMENT FOR MACRO PHOTOGRAPHY

› Close-up attachment lenses

Close-up attachment lenses are simple magnifying lenses that screw into the filter thread of the lens. They are light, convenient, inexpensive, and fully compatible with the camera's exposure and focusing systems. For best results, it's recommended to use them with prime lenses (see page 188).

Nikon produces six close-up attachment lenses—see the table below.

› Extension tubes

Extension tubes, also known as extension rings, are another simple, economical, way to extend a lens's close-focusing capabilities. The tubes, mounting between the lens and the camera, decrease the minimum focusing distance, and increase the magnification factor. They are light, compact, and easy to carry and attach.

Nikon produces four extension rings, but all are of an elderly design and inordinately expensive. A set of three compatible tubes (12mm, 20mm, and 36mm) from Kenko costs little more than a single Nikon tube. They fully support metering and auto-exposure. They don't support autofocus with all lenses, but that's a minor issue in most macro work.

Warning!

Some lenses are incompatible with accessories like extension tubes and bellows. Check the lens's manual.

PRODUCT NUMBER	ATTACHES TO FILTER THREAD	RECOMMENDED FOR USE WITH
0, 1	52mm	Standard lenses
3T, 4T	52mm	Short telephoto lenses
5T, 6T	62mm	Telephoto lenses

» MACRO LENSES

› Bellows

Like extension tubes, bellows extend the spacing between the lens and the camera body, but offer a greater range of extension. However, they are expensive, heavy, and slow to set up—they're for the experienced macro specialist only.

› Reversing rings

Also known as reverse adapters or inversion rings, these allow lenses to be mounted in reverse, allowing them to focus much more closely than when used normally. They are ideally used with a prime lens. Nikon's inversion ring BR-2A fits a 52mm filter thread.

True macro lenses achieve reproduction ratios of 1:1 or better and are optically optimized for close-up work, although they are normally very capable for general photography too. This is certainly true of Nikon's Micro Nikkor lenses, of which there are currently five. Two of them are specifically designed for the DX format, and will be described first, but the others work just as well on the D5500.

The most recent addition to the range is the 40mm f/2.8G AF-S DX Micro Nikkor. It's Nikon's lightest, and least expensive, macro lens, and works well as a standard lens too. However, its working distance at 1:1 reproduction ratio is just 6in. (16cm), leaving very little room between the subject and the front of the lens.

The 85mm f/3.5G ED VR AF-S DX Micro Nikkor also achieves 1:1 reproduction— with approximately double the working

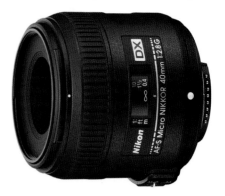

40MM F/2.8G AF-S DX MICRO NIKKOR »

distance—and has VRII, internal focusing, and ED glass.

The 60mm f/2.8G ED AF-S Micro Nikkor is an upgrade to the previous 60mm f/2.8D. Advances include ED glass for superior optical quality and Silent Wave Motor for ultra-quiet autofocus.

The 105mm f/2.8G AF-S VR Micro Nikkor was the world's first macro lens with VR (Vibration Reduction). It also features internal focusing, ED glass, and Silent Wave Motor.

The most venerable of the range, the 200mm f/4D ED-IF AF Micro Nikkor, is ideal when shooting the animal kingdom, as its longer working distance reduces the risk of disturbing your subject. However, it lacks a built-in motor and so can't autofocus with the D5500; this may be an issue when shooting lively animals. With static subjects, manual focus is easy.

Note:
There's no doubt that Nikon's macro lenses are excellent—but the lens used for all the close-up illustrations in this book is a 100mm Tokina.

› Vibration Reduction

As the slightest camera shake is magnified at high reproduction ratios, VR (Vibration Reduction) technology is extremely welcome, allowing you to employ shutter speeds of up to four stops slower than otherwise possible. However, it can't compensate for movement of the subject. It's also almost impossible to avoid swaying slightly when handholding, and at close range the slightest change in subject-to-camera distance can completely ruin the focus. In macro shooting, VR is no substitute for care and a good tripod.

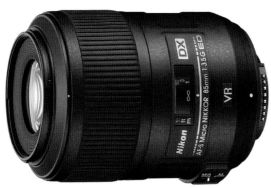

85MM F/3.5G ED VR AF-S DX **«**
MICRO NIKKOR

6 MOVIES

Nikon pioneered DSLR movie-making with the D90 (2008). For many, the true purpose of the SLR is to shoot stills and its ergonomics are still best for this, but the addition of video is no mere sideshow. Professional movie makers have embraced DSLRs because their large sensors deliver image quality that's superior—and just plain different—to standard camcorders, while photojournalists welcome the ability to shoot high-quality stills and video on the same camera. However, still photography and movies are very different media, requiring distinctly different approaches for best results.

» ADVANTAGES

DSLRs in general, not least the D5500, have some real advantages over standard camcorders. One is the large sensor's ability to give very shallow depth of field (see page 92); movie-makers have eagerly embraced this "DSLR look". The large sensor also brings greater dynamic range (page 108) and better quality at high ISO ratings, extending the possibilities for shooting in low light.

Another plus is the D5500's ability to use the entire array of Nikon-fit lenses (see chapter 7, page 188). In particular, it can use wide-angle lenses which go well beyond the range of most camcorders.

Digital camcorders often claim enormous zoom ranges but these are only achieved by "digital zoom", a software function that enlarges the central portion of the image—inevitably losing quality. "Optical zoom" range is what matters,

and interchangeable lenses cover all normal angles of view. The widest range currently available in a single Nikon lens is 18–300mm. Tamron produces a 16–300mm.

THE "DSLR LOOK" »
It's much easier to get really shallow depth of field than with most video cameras.
300mm, 1/500 sec., f/6.3, ISO 640.

WIDE AND HANDSOME »
A 12mm focal length gives a very wide and dramatic view.
12mm, 1/40 sec., f/11, ISO 100.

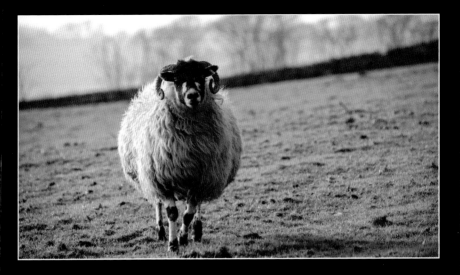

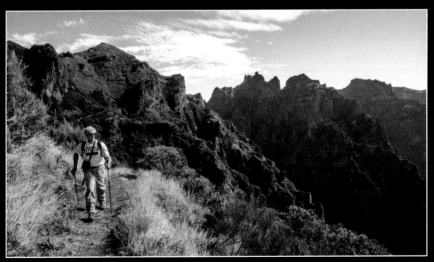

» MAKING MOVIES

› Preparation

Before shooting, select key settings in the **Movie settings** section of the Shooting menu. If shooting in User-control exposure modes, settings such as Picture Controls should also be set in advance.

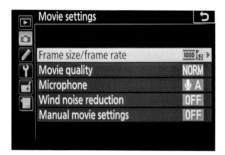

MOVIE SETTINGS ⌃

Frame size/frame rate is a key choice. The D5500 can shoot movies in Full HD (High Definition) quality with a frame size of 1920 x 1080 pixels. Full HD is a general benchmark of video resolution, although the 720p standard (1280 x 720 pixels) looks excellent on most computer screens and mobile devices and gives much smaller file sizes. It has been the norm on *Vimeo.com*, a prime online outlet for quality video.

However, Retina iPads have a 2048 x 1536 display—over 50% more pixels than Full HD. With displays like this becoming common, and with "4K" video (equivalent to around eight megapixels) becoming available on affordable cameras, 720p may look inadequate as time goes on.

Available frame rate options vary according to the image size. Higher frame rates (50p, 60p) allow for half-speed playback for smooth slow-motion. Played back at normal speed they may give smoother results in fast action and panning, and also improve compatibility with future generations of TV. However these frame rates also create larger movie files which can fill up memory cards even faster.

Movie quality sets the compression level; options are **High** or **Normal**. These are equivalent to JPEG quality settings (page 82).

Microphone determines the sensitivity of the built-in microphone (or an external microphone if attached). The options are: **Auto**, **Manual Sensitivity** (in steps from 1–20), and **Off**. You can see an audio-level display while in this menu, which helps to establish a correct setting—which should be sorted beforehand, as you can't change Manual settings while shooting a clip.

Wind noise reduction can be set **On** or **Off**. It applies only to the built-in microphones. Enabling it can indeed reduce the level of wind noise but may also impair the quality of other sound.

If you set **Manual movie settings** to **On**, you can adjust shutter speed while actually shooting a clip in M mode. You can also change ISO settings, not while actually shooting but at least without exiting Live View. By default, **Manual movie settings** is **Off**. When it is, you can dial in changes to the settings but they have no effect.

Whether this is **On** or **Off**, if you're shooting in M mode, you can't change the aperture without exiting Live View.

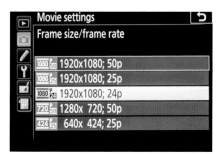

SETTING FRAME SIZE/FRAME RATE IN ⌃ THE MOVIE SETTINGS MENU

Picture Control

In **P**, **S**, **A**, or **M** modes, **Picture Control** should be set in advance; see the Movie Live View options, below.

If you're planning to adjust the look of the movie in post-processing ("grading")

then the Flat Picture Control (page 106) gives most latitude for this, but if you're likely to use the footage more or less as it comes, pick the Picture Control closest to the look you want.

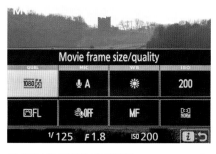

MOVIE LIVE VIEW OPTIONS ⌃

Movie Live View options

A number of useful options can be accessed from Live View—but not while actually shooting a clip—by pressing ◄**⊞**. First, make sure that the Live View screen is showing **Movie indicators** (if not, press **info** to cycle through the screens, as described on page 94). Pressing ◄**⊞** then reveals a specialized active information display including the following options:

Movie frame size/quality

This includes the same options as the **Frame size/frame rate** and **Movie quality** items in the Shooting menu (page 174), but they are laid out differently.

Microphone

This includes the same options as the corresponding item in the Shooting menu (page 174).

White balance

The normal options are available (page 80).

Exposure compensation

This can be set with the multi-selector or touch controls. If Manual movie settings is **On**, this item shows ISO instead.

Picture Control

Normal options are available.

Wind noise reduction

This can be set to **On** or **Off**.

Focus mode

Normal options are available (see below).

AF-area mode

Normal options are available (see below).

The focus modes and AF-area options for movie shooting are the same as for Live View (page 96). If Full-time servo AF (AF-F) is selected, the D5500 will automatically maintain focus during movie recording. Perhaps we should say it will attempt to do so—Live View AF is nowhere near agile enough for fast-moving subjects. It's important to be aware of this limitation. Sometimes you just have to work round it and plan alternative shots that don't push the AF system so far.

In Single-servo AF (AF-S) the camera will only refocus when you half-press the shutter-release button, or tap the subject on screen. Tapping the screen is a good way to shift the focus point quickly, without slow (and possibly noisy) use of the multi-selector, but can cause wobbles if the camera isn't securely held.

Manual focusing is also possible, but can be yet another recipe for wobbly pictures. A tripod helps, especially with longer lenses, where focusing is more critical and wobbles are magnified. Some lenses have a smoother manual focus action than others. The physical design of older lenses often makes them more suitable, with large and well-placed focus rings. There are attachments (which are often expensive) that allow you to control focus more smoothly and precisely.

Unexpected or inaccurate shifts in focus

can be very disconcerting when viewing the footage. Fortunately, refocusing is often not necessary. Using a fixed focus is perfectly viable for many shots, especially when depth of field is good. To employ fixed focus, use AF-S (Single-servo AF), set focus in Live View before shooting the clip, and avoid pressing the shutter-release button while shooting. Or just use manual focus.

› Exposure

In Auto, Scene, and Effects modes, exposure control for movies works similarly to shooting stills. In Full Auto modes, exposure control is fully automatic. In Scene and Effects modes, you can lock exposure level while shooting using **AE-L/AF-L** . This is useful, for instance, to prevent the main subject appearing to darken if it moves in front of a brighter background. You can also apply exposure compensation while shooting using 🄴 and the command dial. The screen gives a rough preview of the effect on the exposure level.

In User-control modes, the usual options apply, but for the most part you can only adjust them in Live View, not when actually shooting a clip. Exposure lock and exposure compensation can be

DRUMMER IN THE DARK ⌄
The D5500 also scores when it comes to low-light shooting.
150mm, 1/50 sec., f/4, ISO 1600.

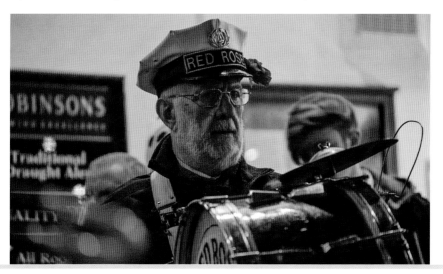

applied as above, but you can't directly change shutter speed or aperture yourself in mid-shot. In fact, to change the aperture in A or M mode you don't just need to stop shooting a clip; you actually need to dial in the new setting then exit and re-enter Live View before it takes effect.

Other than exposure lock and exposure compensation, there's really only one way to directly change exposure settings while actually shooting a clip. This applies in mode M, if you've set **Manual movie settings** option (see page 175) to **On**. In this case, you can adjust the shutter speed "live" while shooting, and see on screen how this affects the exposure level. You can also adjust the ISO level in mid-shot, using **Fn** and the command dial. You must, of course, have **Fn** set to ISO in Custom Setting f1 (see page 124).

While adjustment options are welcome, actually using them while shooting is fiddly. It's hard to avoid jogging the camera unless it's on a very solid tripod, and the built-in microphones may well pick up the sounds of the operations (the command dial is particularly noisy). Another consequence can be abrupt brightness changes in the final footage. It's usually preferable to get the settings right before you start shooting a clip, and then leave well alone.

You can (if the light's good) set shutter speeds right up to 1/4000 sec., but there are inevitable limits to the slowest speed you can select. For instance, if frame rate is 24, 25, or 30, the slowest possible speed is 1/30 sec. If you're shooting 25 frames a second you can't expect each frame to have a ½-second exposure!

Still photography experience suggests that faster shutter speeds give sharper pictures. In movies it works differently. If you shoot at 1/500 sec., you will find that each frame may appear sharp when examined individually, but the clip appears jerky when played. This is because you have recorded 25 discrete slices of continuous action (assuming 25p frame rate). 25 times 1/500 sec. is just 5% of the action. The nearer the shutter speed is to 1/25 sec., the nearer you get to capturing 100% and the smoother the motion appears on playback. One obvious implication to note is that 🏃 Sports mode isn't much use when you're shooting movies.

However, you can't always shoot at 1/25 sec. and at the same time use a wide aperture for shallow depth of field—in bright conditions, even at ISO 100, you'll probably need f/16. Sometimes you need to compromise, although a neutral density filter (page 213) can come in handy.

Tip

*The indicated shutter speed on screen during shooting isn't always correct. In P or A modes the camera may indicate that it's setting a shutter speed such as ½ sec. or even longer, even though these are "forbidden" for movie shooting. Similarly, in S mode, you can dial in "forbidden" shutter speeds. The only way to be absolutely sure what shutter speed you're shooting with is to use mode M with **Manual movie settings** turned **On**.*

› Sound

The D5500's built-in microphone gives modest quality stereo output. It is liable to pick up any sounds you make during operation (focusing, zooming, even breathing). You always have the option to add a new soundtrack later. However, this is difficult if your film includes people speaking (although "post-syncing" is standard practice in Hollywood, especially for musicals). If you want to include dialog or "talking heads", keep subjects close to the camera and ensure that background noise is minimized.

Fortunately, the D5500 also allows you to attach an external microphone: plug it into the standard 3.5mm mini-jack socket on the left side of the camera. This overrides the internal microphone.

› Shooting

1) Choose initial settings (exposure mode, and so on) as described above. If using **A** or **M** exposure mode, set the aperture. If using **S** mode, or **M** mode with Manual movie settings **On**, set the shutter speed.

2) Activate Live View by flicking the Lv switch. If necessary, shuttle to the "movie indicators" screen by pressing info one or more times (see page 94).

3) Check framing and initial exposure level (possibly taking a still frame or very short clip as a test). Check sound levels.

4) Set focus by half-pressure on the shutter-release button, tap the subject on screen, or focus manually.

5) Press ⊙ to start recording the movie. **REC** appears on the monitor screen while recording, and an indicator shows the maximum remaining shooting time.

6) To stop recording, press ⊙ again.

7) Exit Live View by flicking Lv .

If a still frame isn't quite right, you can review it, change position or settings, and be ready to reshoot within seconds. To shoot and review even a short movie clip eats up much more time, and you may not get a second chance anyway; so think ahead and aim to get shooting position, framing, and camera settings right beforehand. A short test clip can help to verify these. If you're planning to pan or zoom, you can do a dry run in Live View before shooting for real.

If you're new to the complexities of movies, keep it simple. Do one thing at a time; don't try zooming, panning, and focusing simultaneously. Many subjects can be filmed with a fixed camera: waterfalls, birds at a feeder, musicians playing, and loads more. Equally, you can become familiar with camera movements shooting static subjects: try panning across a wide landscape or zooming in from a broad cityscape to a detail of a single building.

THE MOVIE RECORD BUTTON ⌄

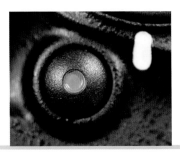

› Handling

The tilting screen improves the D5500's handling for movie shooting, but the overall balance of a DSLR still makes handheld shooting awkward.

It's impossible to overstress the importance of a tripod for shooting decent movies. Vibration Reduction (VR) lens technology can counteract short-frequency shake, but does nothing to eliminate slower (and often larger) wobbles. Of course, even "real" movie directors sometimes use handheld cameras to create a specific feel, but in a controlled way and for deliberate effect.

Using a tripod, or other suitable camera support, is the simplest way to give movie clips a polished, professional look. If one isn't available, look for other alternatives. A beanbag (page 215) is great for static shots. If you have to handhold, try to brace your elbows on your knees or on a solid surface.

A standard tripod with a pan-and-tilt head is fine to start with. For best results, especially when panning, dedicated video tripods (or just tripod heads) are specifically designed to move smoothly.

When a tripod isn't practicable, there are many accessory grips and stabilizers to improve handling and stability, including smaller versions of the legendary Steadicam.

› Panning

The panning shot is a movie-maker's staple, but it's easier to do it badly than well. Often essential for following moving subjects, it's also very effective with static subjects—for instance, sweeping across a vast panorama. Handheld panning may be acceptable when following a moving subject, but a wobbly pan across a grand landscape will definitely grate. Sometimes there really is no substitute for a tripod—and make sure it's properly leveled, or you may start panning with the camera aimed at the horizon but finish seeing nothing but ground or sky. Hurried panning can irritate the viewer and make the shot hard to "read": keep it slow and steady. Smooth panning is easiest with video tripods. With care you can do a reasonable job using a standard model, but it's harder to maintain a consistent rate of panning.

MOUNTAIN RAILWAY ⌄
When panning on a tripod, get it leveled correctly in advance, so we can get an accurate impression of the steepness of this railway.
34mm, 1/125 sec., f/8, ISO 200.

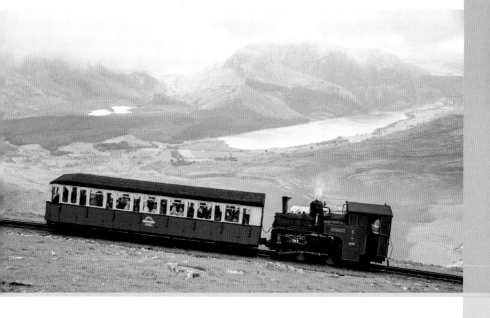

6

With moving subjects, the speed and direction of panning is dictated by the need to keep the subject in frame. Accurate tracking of fast-moving subjects is challenging and takes practice.

HORSE AND CARRIAGE ☙

This is potentially a classic panning shot, but very tricky to follow neatly when handholding. Slow movement isn't necessarily easier to follow. *24mm, 1/80 sec., f/9, ISO 100.*

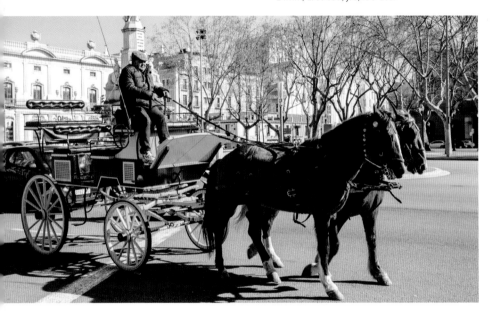

› Zooming

The zoom is another fundamental technique. Moving from a wide view to a tighter one is zooming in, the converse zooming out. As ever, forward planning makes all the difference—consider how the shot will look at both extremes. When zooming in to a specific subject, check it's central in the frame. No DSLR lens has the extreme zoom range of some camcorder lenses but, more seriously, it's hard to achieve a really smooth, even-paced zoom action. Practice helps: mounting the camera on a solid tripod helps even more. What would really help would be a powered zoom, but no current SLR lenses offer this feature. Nikon already makes power-zoom lenses for its Nikon 1 mirrorless cameras, so who knows what may be in store?

When zooming, remember that depth of field (see page 92) decreases toward the telephoto end of the range. Your subject may appear perfectly sharp in a wide-angle view but end up looking soft when you zoom in. Pre-set focus at the telephoto end of the range.

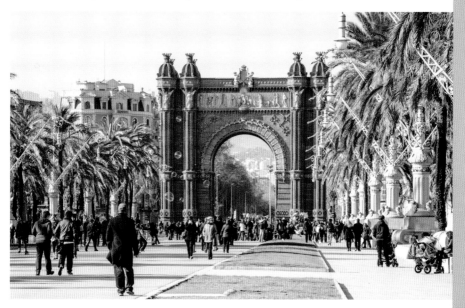

Tip

Video shooting is a real drain on the battery. If you plan to spend a full day shooting movie clips, then you'll probably need several spare batteries, or a mains adapter (page 214) if you have access to mains power.

EXPLORING ⌃

The camera can "explore" a scene like this, either by panning around to see more of the setting or by zooming in for a closer look. The arch at the center of the frame gives a natural focal point on which to zoom.

86mm, 1/250 sec., f/6.3, ISO 100.

> **Lighting**

For obvious reasons, you can't use flash, either as a main light or for fill-in. There are now many LED light units specifically designed for DSLR movie shooting. The D5500's ability to shoot at high ISO ratings is also invaluable.

For fill-in purposes, when shooting at reasonably close range, reflectors are extremely useful. There are all sorts of proprietary reflectors, including ones which fold or collapse to a conveniently small package, but often you can improvise with whatever's to hand, such as a sheet of white card or a table cloth (as long as it's not too windy).

> **Still frame capture**

To capture a still frame during movie shooting, simply press the shutter-release button. This will end movie recording, take the shot (expect a short delay), and then return you to Live View. The resulting image will use your current still image settings for Image quality and Image size (page 82).

You can also extract a still frame from a movie clip you've already shot, but don't expect too much. The image size will be the same as your selected movie frame size (1920 x 1080, 1280 x 720, or 640 x 424 pixels), and motion which appears smooth when playing a movie can look blurred in the single frame.

» EDITING

We've referred to the D5500 shooting movies, but actually it doesn't. Like all movie cameras, it shoots movie clips. A clip, even a collection of clips, is not a movie, only the raw material. Turning this into a movie requires editing.

Digital editing is non-linear, a grandiose way of saying that clips in the final movie don't have to appear in the order in which they were shot. It is also non-destructive, meaning that it does not affect your original clips (unlike cutting and splicing bits of film in the "old days").

During editing, you manipulate preview versions of these clips and the software merely keeps "notes" on the edit. At the end, you export the result as a new movie; this can take a long time to "render".

> **Software**

Nikon now provides movie editing software for Mac and Windows as part of the View NX2 suite provided with the camera. Nikon Movie Editor is a basic, simple, editing package but it handles all the key tasks.

Other, more sophisticated options are available at no cost. Mac users have iMovie, included with all new Macs. The Windows equivalent is Windows Movie Maker, part of Windows Essentials 2012, a free download from *windows.microsoft*.

com. A more advanced (but not free) option, for both platforms, is Adobe Premiere Elements.

All these apps make it easy to trim and reorder your original clips. Instead of simply cutting instantaneously between shots, you can apply transitions such as dissolves, wipes, and fades. You can also adjust the look of any clip or segment of the movie; as well as basic controls for brightness, color, and so forth, you can add a range of special effects.

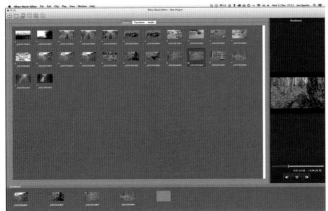

NIKON MOVIE EDITOR «

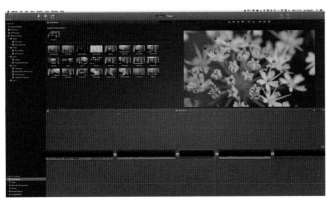

iMOVIE «

You can also add other media, such as still photos and sound. You can insert stills individually at appropriate points or create slide shows within the main movie. Effects and transitions can give slide shows a more dynamic feel.

It's equally straightforward to add a new soundtrack, such as a voiceover or music, to part or all of the movie. Picking a piece of music can determine the length of your finished movie, and changes of key or rhythm will suggest changes of pace or mood in the edit too.

Last but not least, you can also add titles and captions.

› Taking it further

There's far more to movie-making than we can cover in a single chapter. A useful next step would be *Understanding HD Video* by Chiz Dakin, from this publisher.

Tips

Effects and transitions are great fun—and non-destructive editing means you can experiment to your heart's content—but, for the sake of the audience, keep them to a limited selection in the final version.

Unless you created them yourself, still photos, music, and other media are someone else's copyright. Even legitimately purchasing and downloading a digital track does not give you the right to use it in a public performance (showing your movie to a live audience or online). Using unlicenced music can get your video barred by YouTube. Look for open-source material or get the copyright owner's permission to use their work.

SHALL WE DANCE? »
Good quality at high ISO settings is absolutely vital for subjects like this.
18mm, 1/40 sec., f/4.5, ISO 3200.

FLYING THE FLAG »
Detail shots, especially ones with plenty of movement, are really useful for adding variety and change of pace to your movie.
125mm, 1/500 sec., f/7.1, ISO 100.

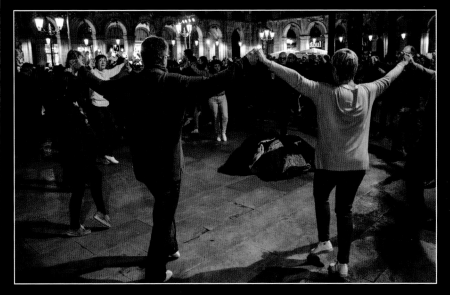

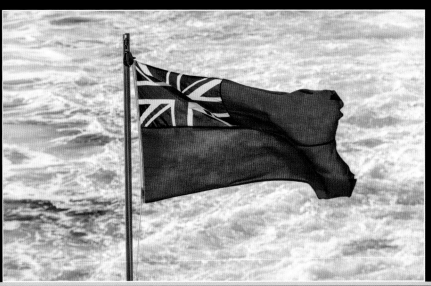

7 LENSES

One of the (many) benefits of a DSLR like the D5500 is its ability to use a vast range of lenses, including Nikon's own legendary system, as well as lenses from other makers. The Nikon F lens mount was introduced in 1959. It has developed significantly, but most Nikkor lenses will still mount happily on the D5500.

» USING OLDER LENSES

When older lenses are used on the D5500, important functions may be lost. In particular, autofocus is only available with lenses with a built-in motor. Suitable Nikon lenses are designated AF-I or AF-S. Check carefully when considering lenses from independent makers (for instance, with Sigma lenses, look for the "HSM" tag).

Other AF lenses with a built-in CPU will support some or all of the camera's metering functions and exposure modes, but will require manual focusing.

Older lenses without a built-in CPU, such as AI and AI-S types, can be attached, but the camera's metering will not operate. You'll need to use exposure mode M; set aperture and shutter speed using an external meter or by trial and error, and use Image review (pages 100 and 114) to check exposure. And, of course, you'll also need to focus manually.

CATHEDRAL »
Even a 12mm lens can't fully take in the vastness of Barcelona's unique cathedral. I could have done with a full-frame camera for this shot.
80mm, 1/30 sec., f/8, ISO 400.

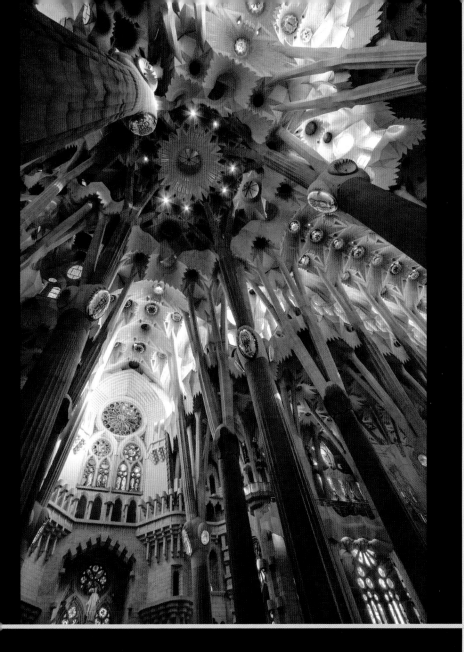

7 » FOCAL LENGTH

Although familiar, the term "focal length" is often used in confusing or even misleading ways.

The focal length of any lens is a basic optical characteristic, and it is not changed by fitting the lens to a different camera. A 20mm lens is a 20mm lens, no matter what.

However, what is often called the "effective focal length" can and does change. I can fit the same lenses to the D5500 or to my full-frame (FX) D600, but the results are different because the D600's larger sensor "sees" more of the image that the lens projects.

Another way of expressing this is to say that the field or angle of view of the FX camera is wider. The angle of view can give another way of comparing lenses. It is usually measured on the diagonal of the frame.

IMAGE AREAS ⌄
This image, taken with a wide-angle lens, shows the same shot using an FX camera (the full frame) and a DX camera such as the D5500 (the red frame) to show the "crop factor" or "focal length magnification factor".

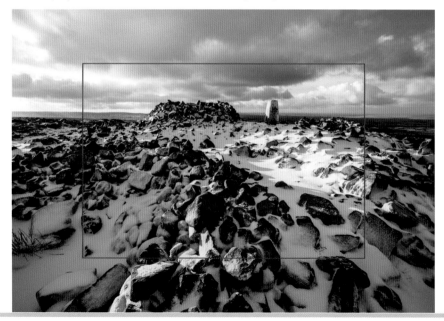

› Crop factor

The D5500's smaller sensor, relative to the 35mm or FX standard, gives it a crop factor, or focal length magnification factor, of 1.5. If you fit a 200mm lens to a D5500, the field of view equates to what you'd see with a 300mm lens on a full-frame camera (e.g. D4 or D600). For sports and wildlife this can be an advantage, allowing long-range shooting with relatively light and inexpensive lenses. Conversely, the crop factor makes wide-angle lenses effectively less wide, which is unwelcome news for landscape shooters. However, this has fostered the development of new ultra-wide lenses, like the 10–24mm f/3.5–4.5G DX Nikkor.

Nikon's DX lenses are specifically designed for use with DX cameras like the D5500. They can be used on FX cameras, but won't cover the full image area of the larger sensor. DX lenses tend to be smaller and lighter than FX lenses of the same focal length. They are listed first in the table of Nikkor lenses on page 204.

The next page shows a series of photographs taken using a Nikon D5500, from a fixed position, with lenses from 12mm to 300mm.

Tip

The lenses on digital compact cameras are normally labeled not with their actual focal length but by their "35mm equivalent"; the focal length that would give the same angle of view on a 35mm or full-frame camera. Throughout this book, and specifically in the shooting details for the photos, the true focal length is used.

Warning!

Very early "non-AI" lenses should not be used—unless modified—as they can damage the camera. A few other (rare) lenses should also be avoided (see Nikon's manual).

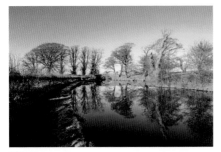

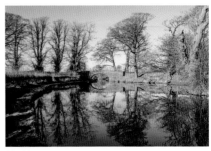

12mm

24mm

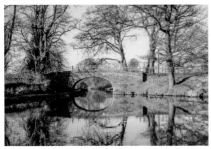

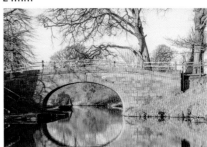

50mm

100mm

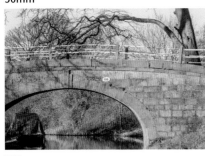

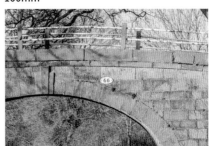

200mm

300mm

FOCAL LENGTH COMPARISON ⌃

Each of these photographs was taken with the Nikon D5500
and a different lens as shown.
1/60 sec., f/11, ISO 100.

LENS ISSUES

› Flare

Lens flare can arise when shooting towards the sun or other bright light sources. Caused by reflections within the lens, it may produce a string of colored blobs or a more general "veiling" effect.

Advanced lens coatings help reduce flare, as does keeping lenses and filters clean. Even so, when the sun's directly in shot, some flare may be inescapable. You can sometimes mask the sun, perhaps behind a tree.

If the sun isn't actually in shot, you can shield the lens. A good lens hood is essential, but may need to be supplemented with a piece of card, a map, or your hand. This is easier when using a tripod; otherwise it requires assistance, or one-handed shooting. Check carefully to see if the flare has gone—and that the shading object hasn't crept into shot.

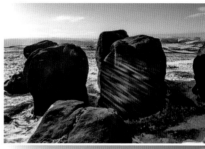

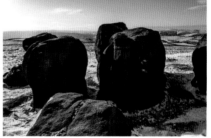

ELIMINATING FLARE ⌃
The flare in the first shot is pretty disastrous, but was eliminated in the second by carefully shading the lens.
15mm, 1/250 sec., f/11, ISO 100.

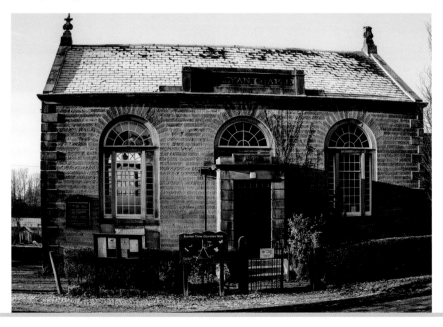
(Large "7" chapter number in top-left margin)

› Distortion

Distortion makes lines that are really straight appear curved in the image. Distortion is usually worst with zoom lenses, especially at the extremes of the zoom range. When straight lines bow outwards, it's called barrel distortion; when they bend inwards it's pincushion distortion. Distortion often goes unnoticed when shooting natural subjects with no straight lines, but can still rear its ugly head when level horizons appear in landscape or seascape images.

Distortion can be corrected using **Auto Distortion Control** in the Shooting menu (page 119) (compatible lenses only), or rectified later using **Distortion Control** in the Retouch menu, or in post-processing. All these methods crop the image.

› Chromatic aberration

Chromatic aberration occurs when light of different colors is focused in slightly

DISTORTION ⌄
Distortion was exaggerated in post-processing. *50mm, 1/100 sec., f/11, ISO 200.*

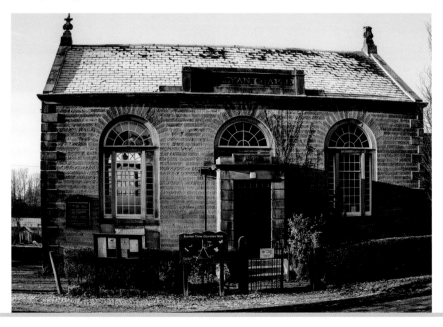

different places on the sensor, and appears as colored fringing when images are examined closely. There is some built-in correction during processing of JPEG images. Aberration can also be corrected in post-processing; with RAW images this is the only option.

aperture, but it should reduce on stopping down. There is built-in Vignette control (see page 119) for JPEG images. It can also be tackled in post-processing. Severe vignetting can arise if you use unsuitable lens hoods and filter holders, or "stack" multiple filters on the lens.

› Vignetting

Vignetting is a darkening towards the corners of the image, most conspicuous in even-toned areas like clear skies. Many lenses show slight vignetting at maximum

VIGNETTE ≫
A strong vignette effect was added in post-processing: along with the color treatment, it gives this recent digital shot an antique look. *16mm, 8 sec., f/11, tripod, ISO 100.*

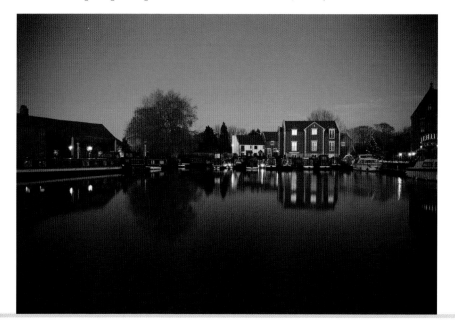

7

› Lens care

Lenses require special care. Dust, dirt, and scratches will all degrade your images. Remove dust with a blower. Fingerprints and other marks should only be tackled with a dedicated lens cleaner and optical-grade cloth. Skylight or UV filters (page 212) can protect the lens, and lens caps should be replaced when the lens is not in use.

BRUSH OFF ⌄
This lens clearly needs cleaning. Always use the proper tools for the job.

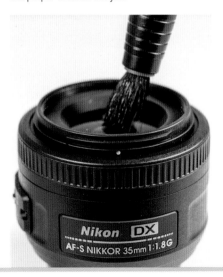

› Lens hoods

A lens hood helps to exclude stray light that may degrade the image and cause flare. It can also shield the lens against knocks, rain, and other hazards. Most Nikkor lenses are supplied with a dedicated hood. Lens hoods are also available separately but Nikon's tend to be disproportionately expensive; third-party offerings may be less than half the price. However, do check that the hood in question is compatible with the lens—try before you buy, taking test shots to check there's no vignetting (see page 195).

HOOD LIFE ⌄
For many professionals, lens hoods—not caps or filters—are the first line of defence. This one shows a few scars!

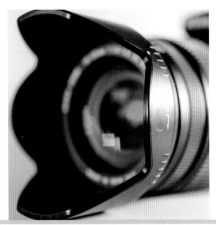

» STANDARD LENSES

In 35mm film photography and full-frame digital, a 50mm lens is called standard, as its field of view is held to approximate that of the human eye; this is debatable, but the label has stuck. Because of the crop factor of the D5500, the equivalent lens is around 35mm. Standard lenses are typically light, simple, and have wide maximum apertures. Zoom lenses whose range includes this focal length are often referred to as "standard zooms".

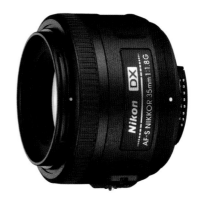

STREET VIEW ⮟
Standard lenses are handy for street photography.
35mm, 1/100 sec., f/9, ISO 100.

35MM F/1.8G AF–S DX NIKKOR ⮝

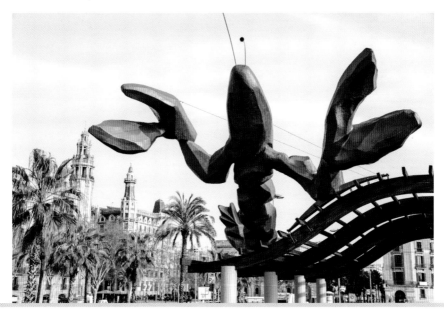

7 » WIDE-ANGLE LENSES

A wide-angle lens is really any lens wider than a standard lens; for the D5500 this means any lens shorter than 35mm. Wide-angle lenses are valuable for working close to subjects or bringing foregrounds into greater prominence. They lend themselves both to photographing expansive scenic views and to working in cramped spaces where you can't step back to "get more in". Because of the D5500's crop factor, a lens like an 18mm, once regarded as "super-wide", gives a less extreme angle of view. This has promoted the development of a new breed of even wider lenses like Nikon's 10-24mm and Sigma's 10-20mm offerings.

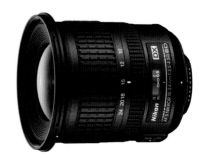

10-24MM F/3.5-4.5G DX NIKKOR ⌃

LANDSCAPE ⌄
Wide-angle lenses work well for landscapes when they are used to emphasise the foreground.
12mm, 1/100 sec., f/11, ISO 100.

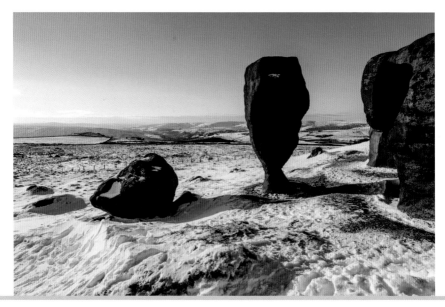

» TELEPHOTO LENSES

Telephoto lenses, often simply called long lenses, give a narrow angle of view. They are mostly employed where working distances need to be longer, as in wildlife and sports photography, but have many other uses, such as singling out small and/or distant elements in a landscape. Moderate telephoto lenses (around 60–90mm with the D5500) are favored for portrait photography, because the greater working distance gives a natural-looking result and is more comfortable for nervous subjects.

When using telephoto lenses, depth of field tends to be narrow. This is often welcome in portraiture, wildlife, and sport, as it concentrates attention on the subject by throwing backgrounds out of focus. Longer lenses can be heavy, bulky, and

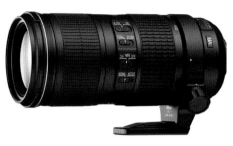

70-200MM F/4G ED AF-S VR NIKKOR ≈

hard to handhold comfortably. Their narrow view also magnifies any shake or wobble. High shutter speeds and/or tripods or other camera support are often required. Nikon's Vibration Reduction (VR) technology also mitigates the effects of camera shake, but can slow down the maximum frame rate, which sports shooters in particular need to recognize.

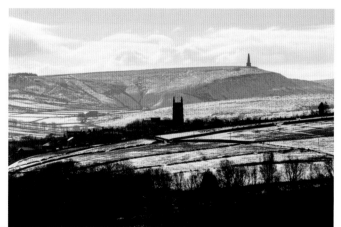

TOWERS «
Telephoto lenses are useful for picking out details in a landscape. *160mm, 1/400 sec., f/11, ISO 100.*

Teleconverters are supplementary units which fit between the main lens and the camera body, and magnify the focal length of the main lens. Nikon currently offers the TC-14E III (1.4x magnification), TC-17E II (1.7x), and TC-20E III (2x). The advantages are obvious, extending the focal length with minimal additional weight (the TC-14E III, for example, weighs just 200 grams).

However, teleconverters can degrade image quality. This can be particularly noticeable when shooting at maximum aperture. Results should improve when the lens is stopped down to f/8 or f/11. Beyond this, sharpness may tail off again due to diffraction.

Converters also cause a loss of light. Fitting a 2x converter to an f/4 lens turns it into an effective f/8. The camera's

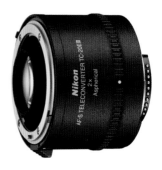

AF-S TELECONVERTER TC-20E III   ☆

autofocus may become sluggish or will only work with the central focus points.

> **Warning!**
>
> **Some lenses are incompatible with teleconverters. Check carefully before buying or using one.**

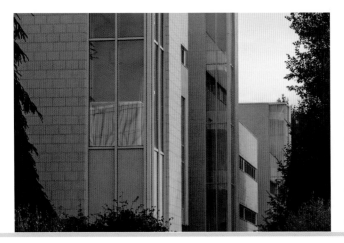

CLOSER VIEW   «
Teleconverters are a convenient and lightweight way to give your lenses more reach when needed.
110mm, 1/400 sec., f/5.6, ISO 250.

» ZOOM LENSES

Zoom lenses have variable focal length, like the AF-S DX Nikkor 18-105mm f/3.5-5.6G, as opposed to prime lenses, which have a single fixed focal length. A zoom lens can replace several prime lenses and cover the gaps in between, scoring highly for weight, convenience, and economy. Flexible focal length also allows very precise framing.

In terms of sharpness and image contrast, there is now little to choose between a good zoom and a good prime lens. Distortion can still be an issue. Most zoom lenses will have a "sweet spot" somewhere in the zoom range where distortion is minimal, but may show discernible barrel distortion at wide settings and pincushion distortion at the long end.

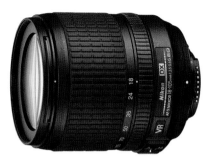

ZOOM-NIKKOR 18-105MM F/3.5-5.6G ≈
AF-S VR

Cheaper or older zooms, and those with a very wide range (e.g. 18-200mm or 28-300mm) still tend to be optically compromised, and usually have a relatively small ("slow") maximum aperture.

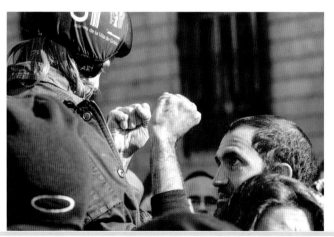

ZOOMING IN «
Zoom lenses give you more options for getting closer to the action.
102mm, 1/640 sec., f/5.6, ISO 400.

7 » PERSPECTIVE-CONTROL LENSES

Perspective-control (PC or "tilt and shift") lenses give unique flexibility in viewing and controlling the image. Their most obvious application is in photographing architecture, where, with a "normal" lens it often becomes necessary to tilt the camera upwards, resulting in converging verticals (buildings appear to lean back or even to one side). The shift function allows the camera back to be kept vertical, which in turn means that vertical lines in the subject remain vertical in the image. Tilt movements also allow extra control over depth of field—whether to extend or to minimize it.

The current Nikon range features three perspective-control lenses, with focal lengths of 24mm, 45mm, and 85mm. They retain many automatic functions, but require manual focusing.

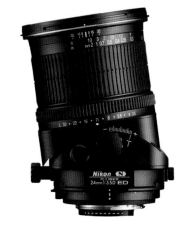

PC-E NIKKOR 24MM F/3.5D ED ⌃

CORRECTING DISTORTION ⌄
PC lenses help to eliminate leaning verticals (left) in shots of tall subjects.
1/15 sec., f/11, ISO 200.

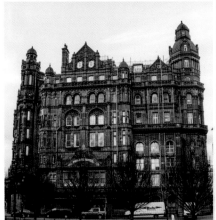
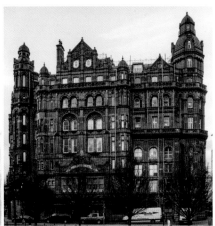

» NIKON LENS TECHNOLOGY

Many Nikkor lenses incorporate special features or materials, usually referred to by cryptic acronyms (as in the table below).

Brief explanations of the main terms are given here.

ABBREVIATION	TERM	EXPLANATION
AF	Autofocus	Lens focuses automatically. Most current Nikkor lenses are AF but manual focus lenses remain available.
CRC	Close-range Correction	Advanced lens design that improves picture quality at close focusing distances.
D	Distance information	D-Type and G-Type lenses communicate information to the camera about the distance at which they are focusing, supporting functions like 3D Matrix Metering.
DC	Defocus-Image Control	Found in a few specialized lenses; allows control of aberrations, altering how out-of-focus areas look.
DX	DX lens	Lenses specifically designed for DX-format digital cameras (see page 10).
G	G-type lens	Modern Nikkor lenses with no aperture ring; aperture must be set by the camera.
ED	Extra-low Dispersion	ED glass minimizes chromatic aberration.
IF	Internal Focusing	Only internal elements of the lens move during focusing; the front element does not extend or rotate.
M/A	Manual/Auto	Many Nikkor AF lenses offer M/A mode, allowing seamless transition from automatic to manual focusing.
NC	Nano Crystal Coat	Said to virtually eliminate internal reflections within lenses, minimizing flare.
RF	Rear Focusing	Lens design where only the rearmost elements move during focusing—makes AF operation faster.
SWM	Silent Wave Motor	Special in-lens motors that deliver very fast and very quiet autofocus operation.
VR	Vibration Reduction	System that compensates for camera shake. VR is said to allow handheld shooting up to three stops slower than would otherwise be possible (for instance, 1/15th instead of 1/125 sec.). New lenses now feature VRII, said to gain an extra stop over VR (1/8th instead of 1/125 sec.).

» NIKON LENS CHART

Optical features/notes

DX lenses

Lens	Optical features/notes
10.5mm f/2.8G Fisheye	CRC
10–24mm f/3.5–4.5G ED AF-S	ED, IF, SWM
12–24mm f/4G ED-IF AF-S	SWM
16–85mm f/3.5–5.6G ED VR AF-S	VRII, SWM
17–55mm f/2.8G ED-IF AF-S	ED, SWM
18–55mm f/3.5–5.6G VR II AF-S (Retractable)	VRII, SWM
18–55mm f/3.5–5.6G AF-S VR	VR, SWM
18–70mm f3.5–4.5G ED-IF AF-S	ED, SWM
18–105mm F/3.5–5.6G ED VR AF-S	ED, IF, VRII, NC, SWM
18–140mm F/3.5–5.6G ED VR AF-S	ED, IF, VRII, SWM
18–200mm f/3.5–5.6G ED AF-S VRII	ED, SWM, VRII
18–300mm f/3.5–5.6G ED VR AF-S	ED, IF, SWM, VRII
35mm f/1.8G AF-S	SWM
40mm f/2.8G AF-S Micro NIKKOR	SWM
55–200mm f/4–5.6G ED VR II	ED, SWM, VRII
55–200mm f/4–5.6 AF-S VR	ED, SWM, VR
55–300mm f/4.5–5.6G ED VR	ED, SWM
85mm f/3.5G ED VR AF-S Micro Nikkor	ED, IF, SWM, VRII

AF prime lenses

Lens	Optical features/notes
14mm f/2.8D ED AF	ED, RF
16mm f/2.8D AF Fisheye	CRC

Angle of view on DX format (°)	Minimum focus distance (m)	Filter size	Dimensions (diameter/length, mm)	Weight (g)
180	0.14	Rear	63 x 62.5	300
109–61	0.24	77	82.5 x 87	460
99–61	0.3	77	82.5 x 90	485
83–18.5	0.38	67	72 x 85	485
79–28.5	0.36	77	85.5 x 11.5	755
76–28.5	0.28	52	66 x 59.5 (retracted)	195
76–28.5	0.28	52	73 x 79.5	265
76–22.5	0.38	67	73 x 75.5	420
76–15.3	0.45	67	76 x 89	420
76–11.5	0.45	67	78 x 97	490
76–8	0.5	72	77 x 96.5	560
76–5.3	0.45	77	83 x 120	830
44	0.3	52	70 x 52.5	210
38.5	0.163	52	68.5 x 64.5	235
28.5–8	1.1	52	70.5 x 83	300
28.5–8	1.1	52	73 x 99.5	335
28.5–5.2	1.4	58	76.5 x 123	530
18.5	0.28	52	73 x 98.5	355
90	0.2	Rear	87 x 86.5	670
120	0.25	Rear	63 x 57	290

20mm f/1.8G ED AF-S	ED, NC
20mm f/2.8D AF	CRC
24mm f/1.4G ED	ED, NC
24mm f/2.8D AF	
28mm f/1.8G AF-S	NC, SWM
28mm f/2.8D AF	
35mm f/2D AF	
35mm f/1.8G AF-S	RF, SWM
35mm f/1.4G AF-S	NC, SWM
50mm f/1.8G AF-S	SWM
50mm f/1.8D AF	
50mm f/1.4D AF	
50mm f/1.4G AF-S	IF, SWM
58mm f/1.4G AF-S	NC, SWM
85mm f/1.4G AF	SWM, NC
85mm f/1.8D AF	RF
85mm AF-S f/1.8G	IF, SWM
105mm f/2D AF DC	DC
135mm f/2D AF DC	DC
180mm f/2.8D ED-IF AF	ED, IF
200mm f/2G ED-IF AF-S VRII	ED, VRII, SWM
300mm f/4E PF ED VR AF-S	ED, SWM, NC, IF
300mm f/4D ED-IF AF-S	ED, IF
300mm f/2.8G ED VR II AF-S	ED, VRII, NC, SWM
400mm f/2.8G ED VR AF-S	ED, IF, VRII, NC
400mm f2.8E FL ED VR AF-S	
400mm f/2.8D ED-IF AF-S II	ED, SWM

Angle of view on DX format (°)	Minimum focus distance (m)	Filter size	Dimensions (diameter/length, mm)	Weight (g)
70	0.2	77		355
70	0.25	62	69 x 42.5	270
61	0.25	77	83 x 88.5	620
61	0.3	52	64.5 x 46	270
53	0.25	67	73 x 80.5	330
53	0.25	52	65 x 44.5	205
44	0.25	52	64.5 x 43.5	205
44	0.25	58	72 x 71.5	305
44	0.3	67	83 x 89.5	600
31.3	0.45	58	72 x 52.5	185
31.3	0.45	52	63 x 39	160
31.3	0.45	52	64.5 x 42.5	230
31.3	0.45	58	73.5 x 54	280
27.3	0.58	72	85 x 70	385
18.5	0.85	77	86.5 x 84	595
18.5	0.85	62	71.5 x 58.5	380
18.5	0.8	67	80 x 73	350
15.2	0.9	72	79 x 111	640
12	1.1	72	79 x 120	815
9.1	1.5	72	78.5 x 144	760
8.2	1.9	52	124 x 203	2930
5.2	1.4	77	89 x 147.5	755
5.2	1.45	77	90 x 222.5	1440
5.2	2.2	52	124 x 267.5	2900
4	2.9	52	159.5 x 368	4620
4	3.8	52	160 x 352	4800

500mm f/4G ED VR AF-S	IF, ED, VRII, NC
600mm f/4G ED VR AF-S	ED, IF, VRII, NC
800mm f/5.6E FL ED VR AF-S	ED, NC, SWM, FL
AF zoom lenses	
14–24mm f/2.8G ED AF-S	IF, ED, SWM, NC
16–35mm f/4G ED VR	NC, ED, VR
17–35mm f/2.8D ED-IF AF-S	IF, ED, SWM
18–35mm f/3.5–4.5G ED AF-S	ED, SWM
24–70mm f/2.8G ED AF-S	ED, SWM, NC
24–85mm f/2.8–4D IF AF	IF
24–85mm f/3.5–4.5G ED VR AF-S	ED, VRII, SWM
24–120mm f/4G ED-IF AF-S VR	ED, SWM, NC, VRII
28–300mm f/3.5–5.6G ED VR	ED, SWM
70–200mm f/2.8G ED-IF AF-S VRII	ED, SWM, VRII
70–200mm f/4G ED AF-S VRIII	ED, IF, SWM, NC, VRIII
70–300mm f/4.5–5.6G AF-S VR	ED, IF, SWM, VRII
80–400mm f/4.5–5.6D ED VR AF-S	ED, VR, NC
200–400mm f/4G ED-IF AF-S VRII	ED, NC,VRII, SWM
Macro lenses	
60mm f/2.8G ED AF-S Micro	ED, SWM, NC
105mm f/2.8G AF-S VR Micro	ED, IF, VRII, NC, SWM
200mm f/4D ED-IF AF Micro	ED, CRC
Perspective-control lenses	
24mm f/3.5D ED PC-E (manual focus)	ED, NC
45mm f/2.8D ED PC-E (manual focus)	ED, NC
85mm f/2.8D ED PC-E (manual focus)	ED, NC

Angle of view on DX format (°)	Minimum focus distance (m)	Filter size	Dimensions (diameter/length, mm)	Weight (g)
3.1	4	52	139.5 x 391	3880
2.4	5	52	166 x 445	5060
2	5.9	52	160 x 461	4590
90–61	0.28	None	98 x 131.5	970
83–44	0.29	77	82.5 x 125	680
79–44	0.28	77	82.5 x 106	745
76–44	0.28	77	83 x 95	385
61–22.50	0.38	77	83 x 133	900
61–18.5	0.5	72	78.5 x 82.5	545
61–18.5	0.38	72	78 x 82	465
61–13.5	0.45	77	84 x 103.5	710
53–5.2	0.5	77	83 x 114.5	800
22.5–8	1.4	77	87 x 209	1540
22.5–8	1	67	78 x 178.5	850
22.5–5.20		67	80 x 143.5	745
20–4	2.3	77	95.5 x 203	1570
8–4	2	52	124 x 365.5	3360
26.3	0.185	62	73 x 89	425
15	0.31	62	83 x 116	720
8	0.5	62	76 x 104.5	1190
56	0.21	77	82.5 x 108	730
34.5	0.25	77 x 94	83.5 x 112	780
18.9	0.39	77	82.7 x 107	650

ACCESSORIES AND CARE

Beyond lenses and flashguns, there are many other accessories which can extend the capabilities of the camera. Nikon's system is huge, and third-party suppliers offer even more options.

» ESSENTIALS

Nikon supplies several essential items with the camera. It's well worth considering the value of spares (notably spare batteries) and upgrades (for instance, for the strap). Small items like the body cap (BF-1A or BF-1B) and hotshoe cover (BS-1) are easily misplaced but cheap to replace.

› EN-EL14a battery

While the camera's battery life is good, it can't hurt to keep a fully charged spare on hand—especially in cold conditions, when using the monitor extensively, or when shooting movies. Third-party batteries are cheaper but may have a lower power rating. Older EN-EL14 batteries can also be used.

› Strap

The supplied strap is nice if you want to advertise that you're using a Nikon, but even though the D5500 is a light DSLR, the strap isn't very comfortable for extended periods of carrying. There are many alternative straps and other carrying systems. I've recently been impressed by the Slide from Peak Design. It's also much easier to remove from the camera if you want to reduce clutter (e.g. for a long tripod session).

HEAD FOR THE HILLS »

Long hikes to remote locations definitely make you think about what you carry and how you carry it. Forgetting anything essential can end in tears, but there can't be a serious outdoor photographer who has never found themselves without a spare battery, memory card, or tripod attachment at some point in their career.
28mm, 1/250 sec., f/11, tripod, ISO 100.

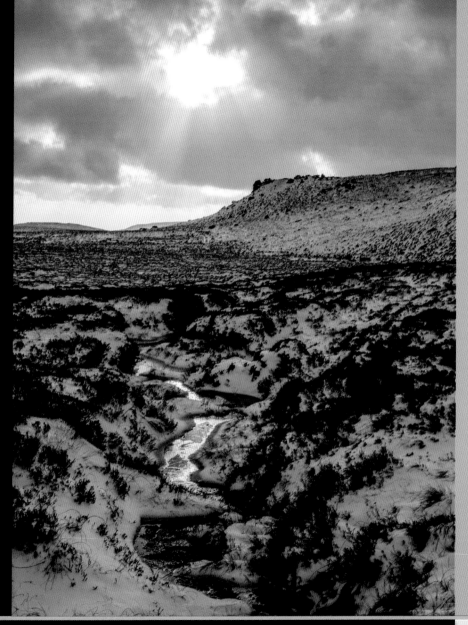

8 » FILTERS

Digital features like variable white balance (page 77) have made many filters almost redundant. Soft-focus and starburst effects, among others, can be added in-camera via the Retouch menu (page 138)—although the starburst lacks finesse. A far wider range of effects is applicable in post-processing.

However, some filters still have value. Many people keep a UV or skylight filter on each lens to protect against knocks and scratches, although many working pros rely purely on lens hoods.

› Polarizing filters

The polarizing filter reduces reflections, cutting glare, intensifying colors, and restoring transparency to water and glass. It can also cut through atmospheric haze and enrich blue skies. Rotating the filter strengthens or weakens its effect, which is strongest when shooting at right angles to

POLARIZER ≫
A polarizing filter can intensify colors and accentuate clouds (as seen in the left side of this composite image).
40mm, 1/15 and 1/80 sec., f/11, ISO 100.

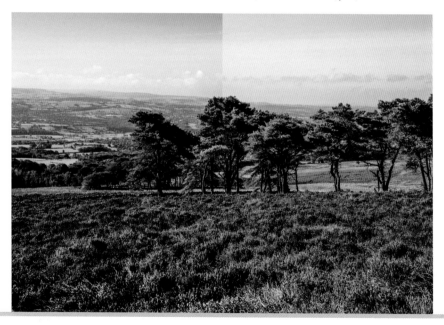

the sunlight. It is virtually impossible to reproduce in post-processing. The effect can vary across the field of view with wide-angle lenses.

› Neutral density filters

Neutral density (ND) filters reduce the amount of light reaching the lens, without changing its color. Plain ND filters allow you to set slower shutter speeds and/or wider apertures. A classic use is shooting waterfalls, to allow a long shutter speed to create a silky blur.

Graduated ND filters have been widely used in landscape photography to compensate for wide differences in brightness between sky and land. However, the straight-line transition can be unpleasantly obvious, especially against irregular skylines. The wide dynamic range of cameras like the D5500 reduces the need for them.

NEURAL DENSITY ⌄
A plain neutral density filter may be useful when you want to use really low shutter speeds.
16mm, 25 sec., f/11, ISO 100, beanbag, ML-L3 remote.

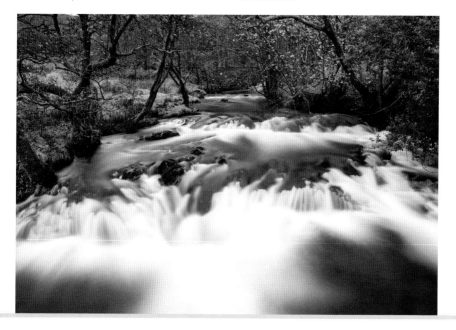

8 » OPTIONAL ACCESSORIES

Like other camera makers, Nikon is often criticized over the price of its accessories. Third-party alternatives may be much cheaper, but take care to source reputable, fully compatible products.

› AC Adapter EH-5b

Can be used to power the camera directly from the AC mains, allowing uninterrupted shooting in, for example, long studio sessions. (A Power Connector EP-5A is also required.)

› Wireless remote control ML-L3

This inexpensive little infrared unit allows the camera to be triggered from a distance of up to 16ft (5m). There are receivers on both the front and rear of the camera. Units like Nikon's WR-1 or Hähnel's Giga T Pro II allow fuller control of the camera.

› GP-1 and GP-1A GPS units

Dedicated Global Positioning System devices provide precise location information (see page 232).

› ME-1 stereo microphone

Greatly improves sound quality in movie shooting (see pages 174 and 179).

› Diopter adjustment

The D5500's viewfinder has built-in dioptric adjustment (see page 24). If your eyesight is beyond its range, Nikon produces a series of viewfinder lenses between −5 and +3 m^{-1}, designated DK-20C.

> **Tip**
>
> *It's usually easier to wear contact lenses or glasses. My prescription is around −5 m^{-1} and I've never had any problem using the D5500 while wearing contacts.*

› Screen shades

Camera LCD screens can be impossible to see properly in bright sunlight. The viewfinder is much better for shooting in bright light, but you still need the screen for Live View, movie shooting, and image review. The best-known maker of accessory screen shades is Hoodman.

» CAMERA SUPPORT

› Tripods

Vibration Reduction (VR) lenses and the D5500's image quality at high ISO settings make handholding fully viable for many shots. Still, dynamic range is best at low ISO ratings, and some shots will always require a solid support. Tripods are essential for serious movie shooting, too (see page 180).

Titanium and carbon fiber combine low weight and good rigidity. They aren't cheap but a good tripod is an investment which should last for many years.

› Monopods

Monopods are light, easy to carry, and quick to set up. They are favored by sports and some wildlife photographers, who often need to react quickly while using hefty, long telephoto lenses.

› Other camera support

There are many other proprietary products and improvised alternatives. It's hard to beat the humble beanbag, which can easily be homemade.

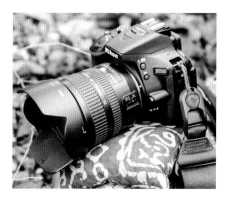

BEANBAG ⌃
A simple, homemade beanbag that has served me well for many years.

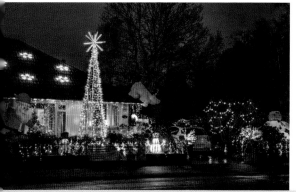

LIGHTS, CAMERA, ACTION! «
Tripods are essential for making movies, and on many occasions for still photography too.
35mm, 20 sec., f/11, ISO 100, tripod.

» CAMERA CASES

A case is arguably essential for outdoor use. A simple drop-in pouch, worn on a waist-belt, is most practical. To carry a larger system, a backpack-type bag is kindest on your spine.

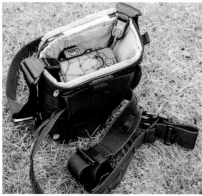

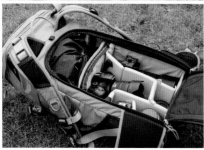

POUCH ⌃
A padded pouch (this one's by Think Tank Photo) combines good protection and easy access.

BACKPACK ⌃
Backpacks—this one's by f-stop—are best for the spine.

» STORING IMAGES

› Memory cards

The D5500 stores images on Secure Digital (SD), SDHC, and SDXC cards. On long trips it's easy to fill up even large-capacity memory cards and prices have fallen, so it's advisable to carry a spare or two.

Memory card performance is measured in two ways: speed rating (e.g. 30MB/s) and speed class rating (e.g. Class 10). Class 4 is adequate for most stills shooting, but for prolonged high-speed bursts or shooting video look for a higher rating.

› Backing up on the move

Memory cards rarely fail but it's always worth backing up valuable images as soon as possible. On longer trips without regular computer access, you can use a mobile device for further backup. Dedicated photo storage devices are becoming rare, supplanted by laptops, smartphones, or tablets.

› Card care

If you lose or damage a memory card before downloading or backing up, your images are lost too. Blank cards are cheap but cards full of images are irreplaceable. SD cards are robust but it's still wise to treat them with care. Keep them in their original

» CAMERA CARE

plastic cases, or something more substantial, and avoid exposure to extremes of temperature, liquids, and strong electromagnetic fields. (Modern airport X-ray machines aren't harmful to cameras or memory cards.)

The D5500 is robust, but it's also packed with complex, potentially delicate electronic and optical technology. A few simple precautions should help to keep it functioning perfectly for many years.

› Basic care

Keeping the camera clean is fundamental. Keep it in a case when not in use. Remove dust and dirt with a blower, then wipe with a soft, dry cloth.

The rear screen may be tough enough to survive without a protective cover, but it will need cleaning periodically. Use a blower to remove loose dirt, then wipe carefully with a clean soft cloth or a swab designed for the purpose. Do not apply pressure and never use household cleaning products.

> ### Tip
>
> *Spots on images can be removed in post-processing. This process can be automated in Nikon Capture NX-D using a Dust-off reference image (page 130) or in Adobe Lightroom.*

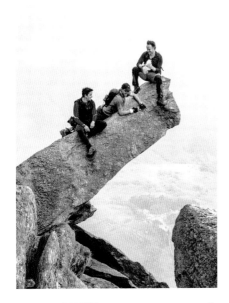

TRAVELING LIGHT ⌃
Make sure that your camera bag is light and comfortable to carry, but also gives all the protection your camera needs—you never know where you'll both end up.
165mm, 1/200 sec, f/8, ISO 400.

› Cleaning the sensor

Strictly speaking, it's not the sensor itself but its protective filter that concerns us. Dust on this will appear as dark spots in your images.

Prevention (page 217) is better than cure but—unless you never change lenses—some dust will eventually enter. Fortunately, the D5500 has a self-cleaning facility. You can activate it manually at any time, or set it to activate automatically when you switch the camera on and/or off. See **Clean Image Sensor** in the Setup menu (page 130).

Occasionally, stubborn spots may remain, making it necessary to clean the filter manually. Do this in a clean, draught-free, well-lit place.

Ensure the battery is fully charged, or use a mains adapter. Remove the lens, switch the camera on, and select **Lock mirror up for cleaning** from the Setup menu. Press the shutter-release button to lock up the mirror. First, attempt to remove dust using a hand-blower (**do not use** compressed air or any other aerosol). If this appears ineffective, consider using a dedicated cleaning swab, carefully following its instructions. **Do not use** other brushes or cloths and **never** touch the filter with your finger. When finished, turn the camera off and the mirror will reset.

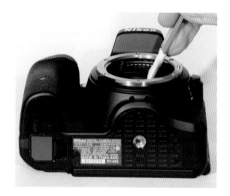

SENSOR CLEANING ⌃
Cleaning the sensor requires great care.

Warning!

The Nikon manual implies that you can clean the reflex mirror with a cloth and cleaning fluid. Do NOT believe it—the reflex mirror is extremely delicate. **Never touch it in any way.** Remove dust from the mirror with an air-blower only.

› Braving the elements

Cold

Nikon specify an operating temperature range of 0–40°C (32–104°F). When temperatures fall further, you can still use the camera, but aim to keep it within the specified range as far as possible. Keeping the camera in an insulated case or under your outer clothing between shots will help keep it warmer than the surroundings. If it does become chilled, battery life can be severely reduced (make sure you carry a spare). In extreme cold, the displays may become erratic or disappear, and ultimately the camera may cease to function. If allowed to warm up gently, no permanent harm should result.

Heat and humidity

Extremes of heat and humidity (Nikon stipulate over 85%) can be even more problematic, and carry more risk of

SAND, SEA, AND SPRAY ⭧
A dramatic image but potentially hazardous for the camera—salt spray is notoriously insidious. Sand, dust, and dirt all require care too.
200mm, 1/2000 sec., f/10, ISO 100.

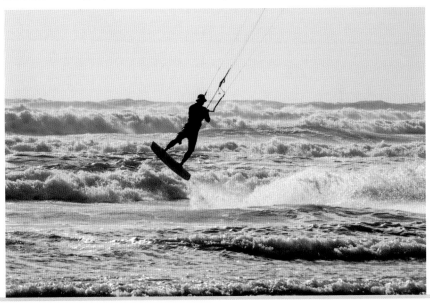

long-term damage. Rapid transfers from cool environments to hot and humid ones (for instance, from air-conditioned hotel to sultry streets) can cause internal condensation. When anticipating such transitions, make sure you pack the camera and lenses in airtight containers with sachets of silica gel to absorb moisture. Allow equipment to reach ambient temperature before unpacking.

Water

The D5500 is reasonably weatherproof, so can be used with confidence in light rain. Keep exposure to a necessary minimum, and wipe regularly with a microfiber cloth. Ensure all access covers on the camera are closed, avoid using the built-in flash, and keep the hotshoe cover in place.

WINTER WONDERLAND

Winter conditions offer wonderful photographic opportunities but can be challenging for cameras.
32mm, 2 sec., f/18, ISO 100, tripod.

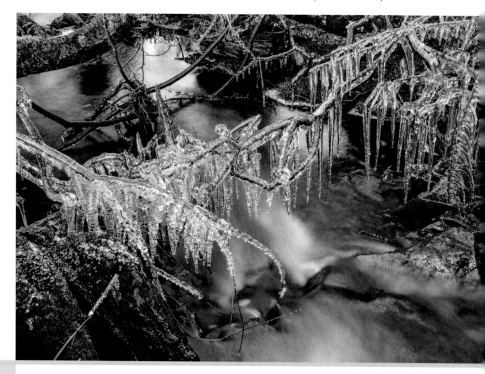

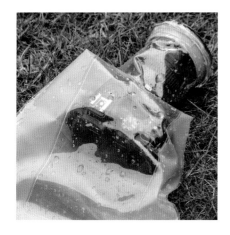

AN SLR CASE FROM AQUAPAC ⌃

Take extra care around salt water. If contact does occur, clean carefully and immediately with a cloth lightly dampened with fresh water, preferably distilled water.

Ideally, protect the camera with a waterproof cover. A simple plastic bag will provide rudimentary protection, but purpose-made rain-guards give better protection and access to controls. Aquapac's reasonably-priced DSLR case is a good match for the D5500 and is rated for depths down to 33ft (10m).

Dust

To minimize spots on images, and the need for sensor cleaning (page 218), try to avoid dust entering the camera. Above all, take care when changing lenses. Aim the camera downward and stand with your back to the wind. In really bad conditions (such as sandstorms) it's best not to change lenses at all. Preferably, protect the camera with a waterproof, and therefore dustproof, case. If dust settles on the outside of the camera, remove it carefully, using a hand-operated or compressed-air blower, before changing lenses, memory cards, or batteries. Keep all covers closed until the camera is clean.

SNOWFALL ⌄
Water protection might well be required here. *200mm, 1/200 sec., f/6.3, ISO 400.*

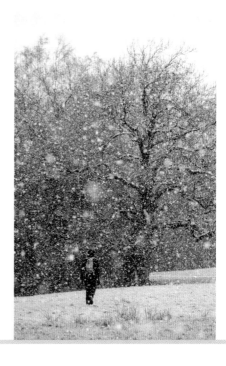

CONNECTION

Connecting to external devices enables you to store, organize, view, and print your images. The Nikon D5500 is designed to facilitate these operations, and a couple of useful cables are included with the camera.

» CONNECTING TO A COMPUTER

Connecting to a Mac or PC allows you to store, organize, and backup your images. It also helps you exploit the full power of the D5500, including the ability to optimize image quality from RAW files.

› Computer requirements

The large file sizes produced by the D5500 are demanding on processor speed, hard disk capacity, and memory (RAM), for which 4GB is a suggested baseline. Fortunately, for most systems, adding extra RAM is relatively easy and inexpensive. Extra hard disk space can also be helpful, as the system will slow significantly when the hard disk becomes close to capacity. Photos eat up hard drive space and videos even more so.

The D5500 supports USB3 for connecting the camera; this is backwards-compatible with USB2 but transfer speeds over USB2 will be slower. You can also use a card-reader (see next page). A CD drive is no longer essential, as the supplied software can also be downloaded from

Nikon websites. Of course there are many other apps available for handling your images and video, as we'll see on page 228.

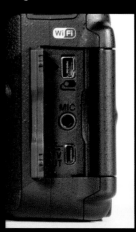

CONNECTION PORTS ON THE LEFT SIDE OF THE D5500

A D5500 CONNECTED TO A COMPUTER »

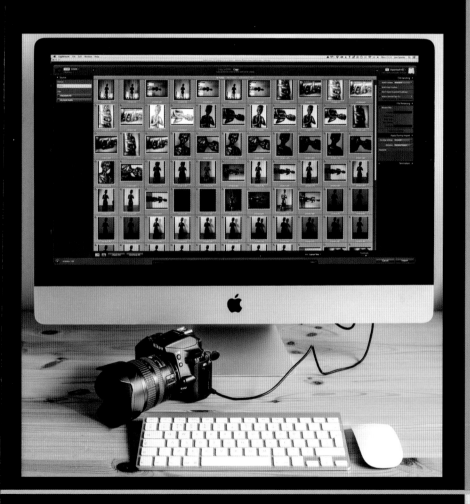

› Importing photos

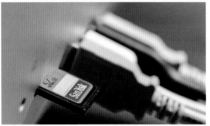

BUILT-IN SD CARD SLOT ON A MODERN IMAC ⌃

The onboard Wi-Fi doesn't let you transfer images to a laptop or desktop. This requires a physical connection, using the supplied USB cable or a card-reader. The latter is usually easier. Many modern computers have built-in SD card slots.

The exact procedure for transferring images depends on the software you are using. Nikon Transfer, supplied along with View NX2, is simple to use and facilitates backup of photos during import, but if you're using an app like iPhoto or Lightroom (strongly recommended—see page 228) to manage your photos, it makes sense to use this for import too. Nikon Transfer may start automatically when you plug in a card or connect the camera. You can forestall this in the dialog box that opens when you install Transfer. If you aren't using Transfer, uninstall it.

Whatever software you use, there are several issues to consider, including whether to backup automatically on import. You also need to decide where on your hard drive(s) photos should be stored. You may also wish to rename files as they are imported.

› Importing movies

The basic procedure for importing movies is the same as for stills. Nikon Transfer will recognize and import them, but you will probably want to store movies in a different folder to still images. Often it's better to import movies through your editing software (see page 184); this keeps all your movie clips in the same place and ensures that the software can immediately locate them for editing purposes.

› Backing up

Initially, each image exists only as data on the memory card. If you transfer images to the computer and format the card for reuse, those images again exist in just one place, the computer's hard drive. Any mishap to that hard drive, whether fire, theft, or hardware failure, could lose you thousands of irreplaceable images.

Many apps offer an option to create backup copies during import, but this

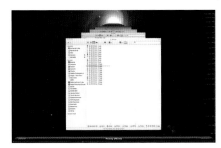

**APPLE'S TIME MACHINE MAINTAINS ⊼
BACKUPS AUTOMATICALLY**

means backing up duplicates, rejects, and
other duds too. You may prefer to backup
after an initial weeding process.

The simplest form of backup is to a
second hard drive; the "gold standard"
requires multiple drives, with one kept at a
different location. Online backup is also an
option. Flickr offers an impressive 1TB, but
commentators have questioned its security
against both data loss and image theft.
Paid, but relatively affordable, services
like Google Drive and Dropbox Pro give
greater security.

› Color calibration

It's a common headache: images look one
way on the camera back, different on your
computer screen, different on a friend's
screen, and different again when printed.
Achieving real consistency across different

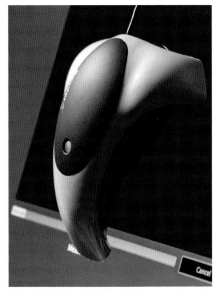

**CALIBRATION IN PROGRESS WITH A ⊼
DATACOLOR SPYDER4EXPRESS**

devices requires color management. This
is a complex subject and detailed advice is
beyond the scope of this book; there's
more in the *Digital SLR Handbook* (from
this author and publisher) and a good
summary at *www.cambridgeincolour.com/
tutorials/color-management1.htm*.

Above all, it's vital that your main
computer screen is calibrated. This might
appear time-consuming but ultimately
saves much time and frustration.

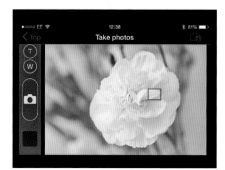

TAKING PHOTOS WITH NIKON WIRELESS MOBILE UTILITY ☆

The D5500 has onboard Wi-Fi. This is undoubtedly welcome for many users, but its capabilities are rather limited.

It will only connect to mobile devices (iOS or Android), not laptop or desktop computers. Wirelessly transferring images to a computer is easy (if slow) with an Eye-Fi card (see page 299), but it's irritating that onboard Wi-Fi doesn't support it.

Further, Nikon's claim that you can "control the camera remotely" is wildly optimistic; you can set focus and trigger the shutter, but can't change any other settings. Finally, it doesn't work with movies.

Still, Nikon's Wireless Mobile Utility is

WATCH THE BIRDY! ☆
Remote shooting minimizes disturbance to shy subjects.
450mm, 1/500 sec., f/4, ISO 400.

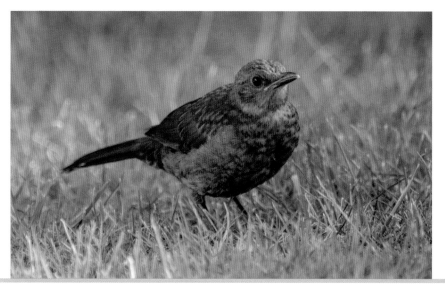

free, simple to set up (especially on iOS devices), and easy to use. The app allows you to view and transfer photos already on the camera, and to take new shots. However, because you can't change camera settings within the app, you need to ensure beforehand that all settings, including Live View focusing options (page 96) are as you want them.

In [WIDE] Wide-area AF or [NORM] Normal area AF, you can focus by tapping the subject on the device screen. You can't zoom in (as you can on the camera) for a precise focus check. However, the preview on an iPad or other tablet is significantly larger than the camera's screen.

› Tethered shooting

Tethered shooting allows you to operate the D5500 from an external device, and to transfer images directly. Nikon's Wireless Mobile Utility is a very rudimentary example. Other apps, like Nikon Camera Control Pro 2 (optional purchase) go much further.

Camera Control Pro 2 allows full control of the camera from a Mac or PC, integrating Live View for real-time viewing. However, it requires either a physical (USB) connection or a very expensive network adapter kit (Nikon UT-1WK)—you can't use onboard Wi-Fi. Lightroom and several other apps also support tethered shooting via USB.

A more affordable solution for wireless shooting is the CamRanger, which supports Live View and control of all the main camera settings. It can link to iOS and Android devices as well as Mac and PC computers. It requires a short USB link to the camera but can connect wirelessly to the controlling device over a range of around 164ft (50m). It creates its own network so can be used anywhere.

› Software and image processing

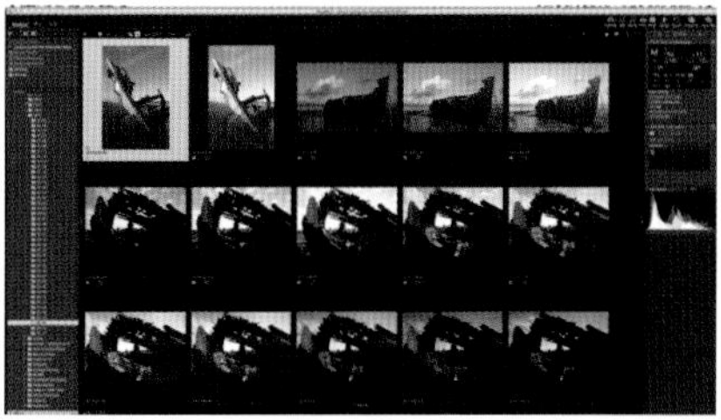

NIKON VIEW NX-i

Most of us want to do more with our images than simply store them. Backing up, printing, organizing, and making them look their best all require the right software.

Software choice depends partly on how you shoot. If you always shoot JPEG images, you may feel little need to tinker with them later, so organizing and cataloging will be your main priorities. If you shoot RAW files, on the other hand, image processing is essential—and gives you great freedom to adjust tone, color, and so on, to your liking.

Nikon software

Early examples of the D5500 came with Nikon View NX2 software, but this has been superseded by Nikon View NX-i (available as a free download). Unlike View NX2, NX-i is purely a browser/organizer. However, it is still neither fast nor intuitive. What's more, to perform even the most basic image-editing or enhancement operations, images must be opened in Nikon Capture NX-D (see below).

Nikon Capture NX-D

Nikon Capture NX-D has recently supplanted Capture NX2. Some changes are welcome, including the price (it's free). Editing is now non-destructive, and batch processing has been improved, so it should be faster and more intuitive. However, many advanced tools have been removed, and it's still no help with organizing and cataloging. I don't recommend it.

Third-party software

The undisputed market leader is Adobe Photoshop. Adobe has recently changed to a subscription model under the Creative Cloud label, which means that the software is continuously updated—but it will stop working if you don't keep up the subscription payments.

Photoshop's feature set is vast, and many users' needs are amply covered by the more affordable Photoshop Elements. It has sophisticated editing features including the ability to open RAW files. Its Organizer module allows you to "tag" photos, assign them to "Albums", or add keywords. Elements is not part of Creative Cloud—you pay once for a perpetual license to use the software, in the familiar way.

Many Mac users have been happy with the free iPhoto, which also unifies organizing and editing. However, Apple has announced that iPhoto (and Aperture) are

ADOBE PHOTOSHOP CC ❯❯

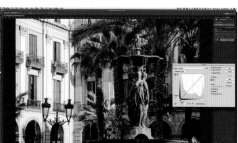

ADOBE LIGHTROOM'S LIBRARY MODULE ❯❯

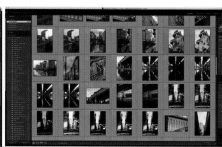

being discontinued in favor of a single Photos app. It's not yet clear whether this will offer advanced features—early indications are not very encouraging.

Complete integration of organizing and editing was pioneered by Apple Aperture (Mac only) and Adobe Lightroom (Mac and PC). The imminent demise of Aperture leaves Lightroom in a near-monopoly position, although this may be challenged by Corel's AfterShot Pro.

Highly recommended, especially if you shoot RAW, Lightroom offers powerful organizing and cataloging, integrated with advanced image editing for seamless workflow. Editing is "non-destructive"—all your edit settings, such as color balance, exposure, and cropping are recorded, alongside the original RAW (or DNG) file. TIFF or JPEG versions, embodying all your edits, can be exported when needed. A Creative Cloud Photography subscription includes both Photoshop and Lightroom.

» EYE-FI

Eye-Fi looks and operates like a conventional SD memory card, but includes an antenna which allows it to connect to Wi-Fi networks, allowing you to transfer images wirelessly. Some Eye-Fi cards also support ad-hoc networks, allowing images to be transferred to a laptop or iPad when out of the range of regular Wi-Fi. However, it will struggle to keep up if you shoot prolifically, especially if you're shooting RAW files.

Eye-Fi software is installed by plugging the card into any Wi-Fi-enabled Mac or PC—that computer becomes the default destination for Eye-Fi upload. The card can then be inserted in the camera; use Eye-Fi Upload in the Setup menu to enable transfers. When out of range of your network, turn this off to save battery power. The card still functions as a regular memory card.

ADOBE LIGHTROOM'S
DEVELOP MODULE ☒

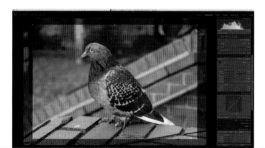

9 » GPS

Nikon's GP-1 or GP-1a GPS (Global Positioning System) units mount in the hotshoe or clip to the camera strap. They link to the camera's accessory terminal using a supplied cable. Other third-party GPS units can also be connected. GPS units add information on latitude, longitude, altitude, heading, and time to the image metadata. This is displayed as an extra page of photo info on playback and can be read by many imaging apps.

When the camera is connected and receiving data from the GPS, **GPS** shows in the information display. If this flashes, the GPS is searching for a signal, and no data is recorded.

Set GPS options via **Location data** in the Setup menu (page 132).

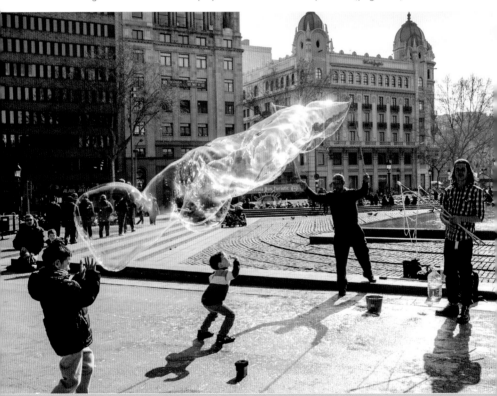

Note:
The D5300 had inbuilt GPS but this has disappeared on the D5500. Cynics might suggest this was simply a cost-cutting measure; a more charitable interpretation might be that it was removed because of its impact on battery life.

› Standby timer

Disable stops the meters turning off and returning the camera to standby. This should ensure a stable connection to the GPS satellites. If you select **Enable**, the meters will turn off after 1 minute, saving battery power. However, next time you take a picture, the GPS receiver may not have time to get a fix, in which case no location data will be recorded.

› Position

Displays the current information as reported by the GPS device.

› Set clock from satellite

The GPS network embodies extremely accurate timing. Setting **Enable** should keep your camera clock bang on.

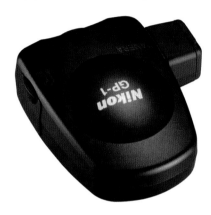

NIKON GP-1 GPS CLIPS INTO THE HOTSHOE ⌃

LOCATION, LOCATION «
GPS is perfect for recording exactly where shots were taken, but keep an eye on battery life.
22mm, 1/320 sec., f/8, ISO 200.

CONNECTION » GPS

THE EXPANDED GUIDE 231

» CONNECTING TO A PRINTER

For maximum flexibility and control when printing, transfer photographs to a computer first. The procedure for printing will then depend on your operating system, imaging software, and the printer you are using. It's now also easy to print from iOS or Android devices.

At times you may still need to print directly from the camera or memory card. The memory card can be inserted into a compatible printer or taken to a photo printing store. Alternatively, the camera can be connected to any printer that supports the PictBridge standard. Only JPEG files can be printed in this way. To print from RAW files, create JPEG copies first (see page 134).

When you connect directly to a compatible printer using the supplied USB cable and turn the camera on, the camera back displays a welcome screen, followed by a PictBridge playback display. You can choose between **Print pictures one at a time** or **Print multiple pictures**.

To print a single picture, select it in the usual way (page 101), then press (OK). This reveals a menu of printing options, including **Page size, No of copies** (1–99), **Border, Time stamp**, and **Crop**. Setting Crop options is similar to using **Trim** in the Retouch menu (page 136). Having set options, select **Start printing** and press (OK). **Print multiple pictures** allows you to select pictures manually. Hold ⊕ and use ▲/▼ to set the number of copies. You can also create an **Index Print** of all JPEG images (up to a maximum of 256) on the memory card. **Select date** prints one copy of each picture taken on selected date(s). **Print (DPOF)** prints images already selected using **Print set (DPOF)** in the Playback menu (see page 115).

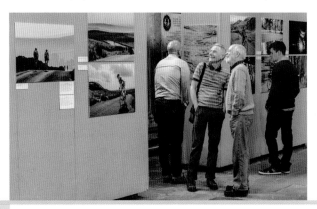

GALLERY　　　　《
Exhibition images will require careful work on the computer before professional printing.

» CONNECTING TO A TV

You can playback photos and movie clips through both standard TVs and HDMI (High Definition Multimedia Interface) sets. They require different cables, but in other respects the process is essentially the same. An AV cable is supplied with the camera.

1) Check that the camera is set to the correct mode in the Setup menu (NTSC or PAL for standard TVs and VCRs, or HDMI).

2) Turn the camera off (important: always do this before connecting or disconnecting the cable).

3) Open the cover on the left side of the camera and insert the cable into the appropriate slot (AV-out or HDMI). Connect the other end to the TV.

4) Tune the TV to a Video or HDMI channel.

5) Turn the camera on and press the playback button. Images remain visible on the camera monitor as well as on the TV and you navigate using the multi-selector in the usual way. You can use Slide show (Playback menu, page 115) to automate playback.

> **Note:**
> A mains adapter is recommended for lengthy playback sessions. No harm should result if the camera's battery expires during playback, but it is annoying.

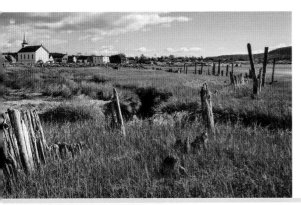

TV SHOW «
A TV can replace the old-fashioned slide-projector and screen as a way of showing images to family and friends. Be selective about what you show, perhaps by using star ratings (see page 115).
35mm, 0.4 sec., f/11, ISO 100, tripod.

» GLOSSARY

8-bit, 14-bit, 16-bit *See Bit depth.*

Aperture The lens opening which admits light. Relative aperture sizes are expressed in f-number (*see f-number*).

Artifact Occurs when data or data produced by the sensor is interpreted incorrectly, resulting in visible flaws in the image.

Bit depth The amount of information recorded for each color channel. 8-bit, for example, means that the data distinguishes 2^8 or 256 levels of brightness for each channel. 16-bit images recognize over 65,000 levels per channel, which allows greater freedom in editing. The D5500 records RAW images in 12- or 14-bit depth and they are converted to 16-bit on import to the computer.

Bracketing Taking a number of otherwise identical shots in which just one parameter (e.g. exposure) is varied.

Buffer On-board memory that holds images until they can be written to the memory card.

Burst A number of frames shot in quick succession; the maximum burst size is limited by buffer capacity.

CCD (Charge-Coupled Device) A type of image sensor used in many digital cameras.

Channel The D5500, like other digital devices, records data for three separate color channels (*see RGB*).

Clipping Complete loss of detail in highlight or shadow areas of the image (sometimes both), leaving them as blank white or black.

CMOS (Complementary Metal Oxide Semiconductor) A type of image sensor used in many digital cameras, including the D5500.

Color temperature The color of light, expressed in degrees Kelvin (K). Confusingly, "cool" (bluer) light has a higher color temperature than "warm" (red) light.

CPU (central processing unit) A small computer in the camera (also found in many lenses) that controls most or all of the unit's functions.

Crop factor *See Focal length multiplication factor.*

Diopter Unit expressing the power of a lens.

dpi (dots per inch) A measure of resolution—should strictly be applied only to printers (*see ppi*).

Dynamic range The range of brightness from shadows to highlights within which the camera can record detail.

Exposure Used in several senses. For instance, "an exposure" is virtually synonymous with "an image" or "a photo": to make an exposure = to take a picture. Exposure also refers to the amount of light hitting the image sensor, and to systems of measuring this. *See* *also Overexposure, Underexposure.*

Ev (Exposure Value) A standardized unit of exposure. 1 Ev is equivalent to 1 "stop" in traditional photographic parlance.

f-number Lens aperture expressed as a fraction of focal length; f/2 is a wide aperture and f/16 is narrow.

Fast (lens) Lens with a wide maximum aperture, e.g. f/1.8; f/4 is relatively fast for long telephotos.

Fill-in flash Flash used in combination with daylight. Used with naturally backlit or harshly side-lit subjects to prevent dark shadows.

Filter A piece of glass or plastic placed in front of, within, or behind the lens to modify light.

Firmware Software that controls the camera. Upgrades are issued by Nikon from time to time and can be transferred to the camera via a memory card.

Focal length The distance (in mm) from the optical center of a lens to the point at which light is focused.

Focal length multiplication factor Because the D5500's DX sensor is smaller than a 35mm film frame, the effective focal length of all lenses is multiplied by a factor of 1.5.

fps (frames per second) The number of exposures (photographs) that can be taken in a second. The D5500's maximum rate is 5–7fps (depending on Image size and power source).

Gamut The range of colors and tones that can be captured in a digital file.

Highlights The brightest areas of the scene and/or the image.

Histogram A graph representing the distribution of tones in an image, ranging from pure black to pure white.

ISO (International Standards Organization) ISO ratings express film speed and the sensitivity of digital sensors is quoted as ISO-equivalent.

JPEG (from Joint Photographic Experts Group) A compressed image file standard. High levels of JPEG compression can reduce files to about 5% of their original size, but not without some loss of quality.

LCD (liquid crystal display) Flat screen, like the D5500's rear monitor.

Macro A term used to describe close focusing and close-focusing ability of a lens. A true macro lens has a reproduction ratio of 1:1 or better.

Megapixel *See Pixel.*

Memory card A removable storage device for digital cameras.

Noise Image interference manifested as random variations in pixel brightness and/or color.

Overexposure When too much light reaches the sensor, resulting in a too-bright image, often with clipped highlights.

Pixel (picture element) The individual colored dots (usually square) that make up a digital image. One million pixels = 1 megapixel.

Post-processing Adjustment to images on computer after shooting. Can cover anything from minor tweaks of brightness or color to extensive editing.

Prime lens Lens with a single fixed focal length, e.g. 50mm.

ppi (pixels per inch) Should be applied to digital files rather than the commonly used dpi.

Reproduction ratio The ratio between the real size of an object and the size of its image on the sensor.

Resolution The number of pixels for a given dimension, for example, 300 pixels per inch. Resolution is often confused with *image size*. The native size of an image from the D5500 is 6000 x 4000 pixels; this could make a large but coarse print at 100 dpi or a smaller but finer one at 300 dpi.

RGB (red, green, blue) Digital devices, including the D5500, record color in terms of brightness levels of the three primary colors.

Sensor The light-sensitive chip at the heart of every digital camera.

Shutter The mechanism that controls the amount of light reaching the sensor by opening and closing to expose the sensor when the shutter-release button is pushed.

Speedlight Nikon's range of dedicated external flashguns.

Spot metering A metering system which takes its reading from the light reflected by a small portion of the scene.

Telephoto lens A lens with a long focal length and a narrow angle of view.

TIFF (Tagged Image File Format) A universal file format supported by virtually all image-editing applications.

TTL (through the lens) The viewing and metering of SLR cameras, including the D5500.

Underexposure When insufficient light reaches the sensor, resulting in a too-dark image, often with clipped shadows.

USB (Universal Serial Bus) A data transfer standard, used to connect to a computer.

Viewfinder An optical system used for framing the image. On an SLR camera, such as the D5500, it shows the view as seen through the lens.

White balance A function which compensates for different color temperatures so that images may be recorded with correct color balance.

Wide-angle lens A lens with a short focal length and a wide angle of view.

Zoom lens A lens with variable focal length, giving a range of viewing angles. To *zoom in* is to change focal length to give a narrower view, and to *zoom out* is the converse.

» USEFUL WEB SITES

NIKON-RELATED SITES

Nikon Worldwide
Home page for the Nikon Corporation
www.nikon.com

Nikon UK
Home page for Nikon UK
www.nikon.co.uk

Nikon USA
Home page for Nikon USA
www.nikonusa.com

Nikon User Support
European Technical Support Gateway
www.europe-nikon.com

Nikon Historical Society
Worldwide site for study of Nikon products
www.nikonhs.org

Grays of Westminster
Revered Nikon-only London dealer
www.graysofwestminster.co.uk

GENERAL SITES

Digital Photography Review
Independent news and reviews
www.dpreview.com

Thom Hogan
Real-world reviews and advice
www.bythom.com/nikon.htm

Jon Sparks
Landscape and outdoor pursuits photography
www.jon-sparks.co.uk

EQUIPMENT

Adobe
Photoshop, Photoshop Elements, Lightroom
www.adobe.com/uk

Aquapac
Waterproof cases
www.aquapac.net

CamRanger
Remote camera control
http://camranger.com

f-stop
Backpacks and accessories
http://fstopgear.com

Peak Design Camera-carrying solutions
https://peakdesign.com

Sigma
Independent lenses and flash units
www.sigma-imaging-uk.com

PHOTOGRAPHY PUBLICATIONS

Ammonite Press
Photography books
www.ammonitepress.com

***Black & White Photography* magazine,**
***Outdoor Photography* magazine**
www.thegmcgroup.com

NIKON D5500
THE EXPANDED GUIDE

FRONT OF CAMERA

BACK OF CAMERA

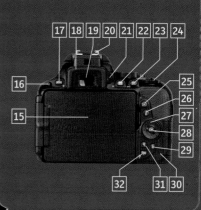

1	Infrared receiver (front)
2	Power switch
3	Shutter-release button
4	Live View switch
5	Mode dial
6	AF-assist illuminator/Self-timer/Red-eye reduction lamp
7	Built-in flash
8	Flash/Flash mode/ Flash compensation button
9	Left strap mount
10	Fn button
11	Mounting mark
12	Lens-release button
13	Mirror
14	Lens mount
15	Vari-angle monitor
16	Infrared receiver (rear)

17	MENU button
18	Eyecup
19	Viewfinder eyepiece
20	Accessory hotshoe cover
21	Diopter adjustment dial
22	Info button
23	AE-L/AF-L/Protect button
24	Command dial
25	Playback button
26	*i* button
27	Multi-selector
28	OK button
29	Delete button
30	Memory card access lamp
31	Playback zoom in button
32	Thumbnail/playback zoom out/Help button

TOP OF CAMERA

33 34 35 36 37

42 41 40 39 38

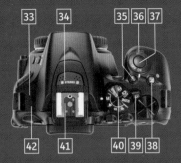

BOTTOM OF CAMERA

50

51 52 53

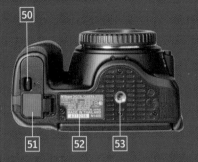

LEFT SIDE

44
43
45
46
47
48
49

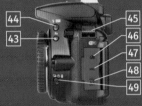

RIGHT SIDE

55
54
56

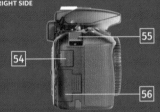

33	Speaker	45	Camera strap mount
34	Stereo microphone	46	Accessory terminal beneath cover
35	Movie-record button	47	External microphone connector beneath cover
36	Power switch	48	USB and AV connector beneath cover
37	Shutter-release button	49	Release Mode/Self-timer/Remote control
38	Exposure compensation /Aperture adjustment/Flash compensation button	50	Battery compartment release lever
39	Live View switch	51	Battery compartment
40	Mode dial	52	Camera serial number
41	Accessory hotshoe	53	Tripod socket (1/4in.)
42	Focal plane mark	54	HDMI connector cover
43	Fn button	55	Right strap mount,
44	Flash/Flash mode/Flash compensation button	56	Memory card slot cover